The United States and Israel

Domestic Determinants
of a Changing U.S. Commitment

Westview Special Studies

The concept of Westview Special Studies is a response to the continuing crisis in academic and informational publishing. Library budgets are being diverted from the purchase of books and used for data banks, computers, micromedia, and other methods of information retrieval. Interlibrary loan structures further reduce the edition sizes required to satisfy the needs of the scholarly community. Economic pressures on university presses and the few private scholarly publishing companies have greatly limited the capacity of the industry to properly serve the academic and research communities. As a result, many manuscripts dealing with important subjects, often representing the highest level of scholarship, are no longer economically viable publishing projects—or, if accepted for publication, are typically subject to lead times ranging from one to three years.

Westview Special Studies are our practical solution to the problem. As always, the selection criteria include the importance of the subject, the work's contribution to scholarship, and its insight, originality of thought, and excellence of exposition. We accept manuscripts in camera-ready form, typed, set, or word processed according to specifications laid out in our comprehensive manual, which contains straightforward instructions and sample pages. The responsibility for editing and proofreading lies with the author or sponsoring institution, but our editorial staff is always available to answer questions and provide guidance.

The result is a book printed on acid-free paper and bound in sturdy, library-quality soft covers. We manufacture these books ourselves using equipment that does not require a lengthy make-ready process and that allows us to publish first editions of 500 to 1,500 copies and to reprint even smaller quantities as needed. Thus, we can produce Special Studies quickly and can keep even very specialized books in print as long as there is a demand for them.

About the Book and Author

Domestic interests and interest groups are significant factors in shaping U.S. policy in Israel and in the Middle East as a whole. Dr. Novik traces the evolution of these elements through the Carter era and Reagan's presidency, projecting their level of importance through the late 1980s. Emphasizing the views of the U.S. public, the Congress, the American Jewish community, and the Christian Right and showing the influence of domestic economic factors and the oil/petrodollar/big-business coalition, he concludes by detailing the areas in which Israel and American Jews can or cannot exercise influence.

Nimrod Novik is foreign-policy adviser to Israeli Prime Minister Shimon Peres. He wrote this study while he was a senior researcher at the Jaffee Center for Strategic Studies, Tel Aviv University, Israel.

Published in cooperation with
Jaffee Center for Strategic Studies

TEL AVIV UNIVERSITY אוניברסיטת תל-אביב

The United States and Israel

Domestic Determinants
of a Changing U.S. Commitment

Nimrod Novik

Westview Press / Boulder and London

Westview Special Studies on the Middle East

Published in 1986 in the United States of America by Westview Press, Inc.; Frederick A. Praeger, Publisher; 5500 Central Avenue, Boulder, Colorado 80301

Library of Congress Cataloging in Publication Data
Novik, Nimrod, 1946–
   The United States and Israel.
   (Westview special studies on the Middle East)
   Includes bibliographies.
   1. United States—Foreign relations—Israel.
2. Israel—Foreign relations—United States.   3. United
States—Politics and government—1981–   . I. Title.
II. Series.
E183.8.I75N68   1985   327.7305694   85-26477
ISBN 0-8133-7133-3

Composition for this book was provided by the author. This book was produced without formal editing by the publisher.

Printed and bound in the United States of America

 The paper used in this publication meets the minimum requirements of the American National Standard for Permanence of Paper for Printed Library Materials Z39.48-1984.

6   5   4   3   2   1

CONTENTS

Tables

Figures

Introduction

A. Background

An astute observer once characterized US-Israel relations as the manifestation of the "gevalt syndrome:" "On any day, one has the impression that (a) the sky is falling down on both states; (b) it will fall down tomorrow; or (c) it fell down yesterday but both governments are too stupid to understand it."[1] This observation seems to fit the early and mid-1980s, as Washington's involvement in the Middle East and Israeli dependence on the United States have entered a new phase.

In the US, the "Vietnam syndrome," a metaphor representing American reluctance to conduct active foreign and security policies in remote areas of the globe, has gradually been giving way to a renewed awareness of the need to actively – even unilaterally – protect western interests against regional and extra-regional challenges. The "Watergate syndrome," which stripped the American presidency of much of the ability to conduct policy by increasing congressional involvement in operational details, seems to have become somewhat muted, although it has not been replaced by a new era of bi-partisanship. Finally, the "Chilean syndrome," which damaged the CIA as an effective arm of US foreign and security policies, has diminished in intensity, allowing the revival of the agency whose effective functioning is so crucial in a complex area like the Middle East.

This phase in Washington's approach to questions of national security comes in the wake of an intensive period of American involvement – implying renewed willingness to undertake expanded commitments – in the Middle East. Interestingly, this was the doing of the Carter administration, which in itself was largely a product of the domestic impact of the Vietnam War and the Watergate Affair. The "Camp David style" of diplomacy – characterized by unprecedented presidential involvement – resulted in increased American commitments to Israel and Egypt, and was rewarded by both the initial Accords and, ultimately, the Israeli-Egyptian peace treaty.

Concurrently, however, a sequence of events in the Middle East region and its periphery put US tolerance to the test. These included: the Soviet airlift of Cuban troops and the expanded role of Soviet advisers in determining the outcome of the Ogaden War between Somalia and Ethiopia (coming, as it were, after a similar exercise in injecting Soviet/Cuban power into another Third World country – Angola – where it was able to determine the outcome of the Civil War); Soviet involvement in the domestic affairs of the People's Democratic Republic of Yemen (PDRY, or South Yemen) and that country's emergence as a major Soviet base on the border of Saudi Arabia; the related – if brief – opening to Moscow in the Yemen Arab Republic (YAR, or North Yemen); the Iranian revolution and the capture of the American Embassy in Tehran; the occupation of the Grand Mosque in Mecca which, coupled with unrest in Saudi Arabia's oil-rich eastern province and with signs of radicalization in several other oil-producing Arab states, demonstrated the potential for instability; the Soviet invasion of Afghanistan; and the Iran-Iraq war.

While even political opponents praised the Carter administration's success on the Egyptian-Israeli front as an achievement of historical importance, its record on these other challenges was far more controversial and was received with far less enthusiasm.

Thus, in the US the awareness of the need to adopt more effective responses to such developments was shared by many. Yet various schools of thought debated the necessary and appropriate remedies. The role of America's friends and allies in sharing the burden of protecting American/western interests in the Persian Gulf-Middle East region has emerged as an important element of the desired formula. One component of it – though hardly the most salient – has been the role to be played by the State of Israel in any suggested scheme for US policy in the Middle East. Views on this issue have ranged along a broad spectrum: from one extreme, where Israel is considered the essential stabilizing center of any framework envisioned for regional security – to the other extreme, where lowering the profile of US-Israel relations and forcing Israeli concessions within the context of the Arab-Israel conflict are perceived as prerequisites and, to some, even as substitutes for an effective formula.

Still, in the mid-1980s, while this debate has yet to be settled, Israel ranks high among US friends and allies as measured by most indices of affinity used in the study of international relations (trade, aid, tourism, cultural exchanges, media coverage, official visits and statements, etc.). Moreover, throughout the 1970s and into the 1980s, Israel has been shielded from potentially damaging

American initiatives by two major actors: the American public and the US Congress. Israel's popularity with both has long served as a deterrent and a barrier against tendencies to pressure and/or punish it, whenever Jerusalem's conduct was judged by the executive branch to be running counter to the US (or Israel's own) national interest. Moreover, the broad support for Israel among the American electorate encouraged legislators repeatedly to use their power of the purse in Israel's favor.

With the inauguration of the Reagan administration these two dams appeared as solid and reliable as ever. Indeed, as Ronald Reagan entered the White House, many observers concluded that the combination of the most sympathetic American president since Israel's independence on the one hand, and an American Congress and public united in their support for Israel on the other, was a guaranteed prescription for four, perhaps eight, years of harmony in US-Israel relations.

Yet, midway through the Reagan administration's first term in office, in the wake of the war in Lebanon (and in an apparent confirmation of the gevalt syndrome), the same observers seemed united in predicting that a serious confrontation between Washington and Jerusalem was inevitable. The administration, they claimed, was convinced that Israel was undermining chances for peace and other US interests in the Middle East. Congress, too, seemed hostile, and was expected to punish Israel by cutting aid. The American public was not expected to object to such measures, as Jerusalem's image was being transformed from that of a peace-loving David to a ruthless Goliath. A proven formula for disaster seemed to be unfolding.

However, within but a few months "strategic cooperation" had replaced "suspicion and hostility" as the more frequently used terms in characterizing US-Israel relations. Even earlier, Congress again raised levels of aid to Israel, while expressions of public sympathy with Israel seemed to reflect the pre-Lebanon war mood. The dams appeared to have survived yet another – most testing – crisis.

This crucial demonstration of the durability of the more basic determinants of US policy vis-à-vis Israel seems to overshadow an equally important – yet rarely recognized – feature of the relationship: changing realities on the American domestic arena have already transformed the basis of the American commitment; they threaten to undermine both dams as well.

B. Thesis

It is the objective of this study to demonstrate that the current phase of the debate over Israel's role in US foreign and security policies is being held at a time when simultaneous changes threaten to alter some of the primary domestic determinants of these policies. These processes of change, if they continue as suggested below, may converge to produce a new setting for the formulation of American Middle East policies – a setting far less compatible with basic Israeli political, economic and security needs.

It is also the contention of this study that while some of these changes will progress independently of developments in the Arab-Israel arena, others are, and will continue to be, affected by perceptions of the conduct of Middle East countries.

Consequently, this study represents an attempt to map and analyze the changing domestic setting for the formulation of American policies that affect Israeli security and well-being. It also seeks to point out the policy-consequences of these changes. The analysis thus focuses on trends and developments in those components of the American domestic arena which are judged to be most relevant to the formulation of these policies.

The first variable addressed is the oft discussed but rarely defined "turn to the Right" in American politics. Identified – for the purposes of this study – in terms relevant to US foreign and security policies, this means greater support for assertiveness both among the public-at-large and in Congress. This is manifested in a general willingness to finance the development of instruments of military power – a major departure from the post-Vietnam era. Yet, the imprint of Vietnam can be readily discernible in another characteristic: considerable restraint in support for the actual use of American forces. The new assertiveness also features a lower threshold of tolerance toward perceived violations of American interests by friend and foe alike. Consequently, this American mood, defined below as Selective Interventionism, entails both the will, however limited, to become involved, and the determination not to be pushed around. As demonstrated below, Israel is excluded neither from the supportive trend of greater involvement nor from the other, punitive, manifestation of lesser tolerance. Indeed, as suggested throughout, Israel's own conduct affects the balance between the two.

4

The second variable is in evidence most clearly in Congress; by definition, however, it characterizes the general public as well. It is the gradual fading of a major ingredient of the earlier American commitment to Israel – the moral debt to the victims of the Holocaust. With the ascent of a generation which either did not reach political maturity during that period or wishes to leave those memories behind, the weight of the historical-moral commitment in determining American policies vis-à-vis Israel has been diminishing. Concurrently, the weight of contemporary moral judgment as well as of more practical considerations has increased. With regard to the former consideration, Israel's image as an admired social experiment has been tarnished by public sentiment toward, and media portrayal of, the less attractive dimensions of Israeli domestic and, more clearly, security policies. Consequently, the latter consideration – translated into perceptions of the balance between the cost of supporting Israeli security needs on the one hand and Israel's utility and contribution to US interests on the other – has gained some importance in determining relevant American policies.

The third major relevant variable affecting the domestic setting concerns difficulties of the American economy, particularly inasmuch as they shape the two dimensions of US economic strength that affect Israel's security: (1) the revitalization of US conventional military capabilities; and (2) the American foreign aid program. On both counts, this study suggests the possibility of hard times ahead.

Lastly, the study addresses the political manifestations of the "decade of OAPEC."[2] Mounting evidence of its ineffectiveness notwithstanding, perceptions of the continued potency of the oil weapon still served, until recently, as a prism through which many Americans perceived Middle East political developments. Yet, even the emerging recognition of a possible evaporation of OAPEC's ability to carry out oil blackmail pales against the growing evidence of the political potency of petrodollars in influencing American political behavior. One manifestation of this new reality has been the emergence of strong competition to the once exclusively influential Middle East Washington lobby – the pro-Israel one.

In sum, this study deals with four major variables affecting the domestic setting for the formulation of US foreign/security policies. The Middle East manifestations of two of them will be

5

affected by Israel's conduct during the months and years ahead. These are (1) American resolve to protect US (and other western) interests abroad – where decisions made in Jerusalem serve as important inputs to the determination of Israel's role as either a helpful ally or an *enfant terrible;* and (2) the changing of the guard in American politics, as the new generation attaches greater weight to Israel's present image and its strategic contribution than to its historical legacy. In this context, the unique role of the American-Jewish community is emphasized.

A third and fourth major variable affect Israel's well-being with equal vigor, yet Jerusalem has little relevancy to their unfolding: (3) the rates of growth, unemployment and inflation in the US and their influence on America's defense budget and foreign aid programs; and (4) the changing global oil market and its impact on OAPEC-US relations.

C. Rationale

The selection of variables stems from several assumptions about the relevancy of specific components of the American political system to the formulation of US foreign and defense policies, particularly with respect to Israeli security and well-being. An attempt to quantify the respective weights of these components within the process is beyond the scope of this study. Moreover, any suggestion of an order of priority among them may be misleading, and may even defeat the purpose of pointing out the centrality of each variable to the formulation of specific dimensions of these policies.

In attempting to focus on the more basic, long-term determinants of the relevant American policies, this study avoids a discussion of the role played by the executive branch. Changing ideological orientations as well as policy objectives, priorities and decisionmaking styles from one administration to another render this variable less predictable within time frames that exceed a single presidential term in office. Clearly, the executive branch is the primary initiator and executor of US foreign and defense policies. The quality and efficiency of these policies are affected by several intra-administration characteristics, including limitations on innovative, independent and responsive decisionmaking, as well as hindrances to implementation stemming from the tendency toward incrementalism, parochial organizational preferences, bureaucratic infighting and "grooved" behavior confined to standard operational procedures (SOPs).[3] Yet, those limitations do not overshadow the administration's advantages over other centers of power in the American political system. The administration enjoys the benefit of the accumulated expertise of foreign and defense career officials; it has an exclusive routine access to classified information and, most important, it is better organized for both decisionmaking and implementation.[4]

This is the case when compared with the other major contender: the US Congress.[5] Characterized by parochialism, localism, relative thinness of expertise and personnel, restricted access to classified information, and defused authority, Congress has had limited success in its competition with the executive branch over the daily management of foreign and defense policies. Consequently, these areas have traditionally been the domain of the executive branch.[6] Yet, in the post-Vietnam era, Congress has become more aggressive and self-assertive on many areas of foreign policy which in themselves appear to be peripheral, but which collectively constitute a major portion of US foreign policy. Although Congress cannot and does not impose a coherence of its own, it does restrain, modify and supplement certain executive branch policies.[7] Most noticeably, these include "economic aid policy, military assistance...and the location of facilities,"[8] as well as elements of the defense budget.[9] Both economic and military assistance constitute major instruments of US policy vis-à-vis Israel. Along with the questions of military facilities and with relevant components of the defense budget, they comprise much of the United States' broader Middle East policy.

Congress' utilization of these very instruments in trying to influence foreign and security policies, makes the American legislature particularly relevant to issues affecting Israeli security. Consequently, changes in Congress that shape its attitude toward Israel's foreign and security concerns warrant careful examination; they may either enhance, or impose further limitations on, the freedom of the executive branch to formulate policies that affect Israel.

Increased attention by representatives and senators alike to the wishes and desires of their respective constituencies, at the expense of congressional leadership and administration preferences,[10] has accentuated the legislators' role as "a barometer of public opinion."[11] However, supportive public opinion may be a significant asset not only to leadership with a local constituency, but to nationally-elected officials as well. Indeed, public support has long been recognized as a major component of a president's "stock of persuasive resources."[12] As a noted scholar/practitioner observed:

> Even the most tough-minded practitioner of real-politik would acknowledge that perceptions of national interests and values are shaped by public opinion....it does provide the immediate context for decisions, it sets some of the rules of the game, and it defines in large measure who will be responsible for the decisions made.... As revealed in countless surveys and polls, ...and as played out in electoral contests, American public opinion does influence foreign policy, but often in very indirect ways.[13]

Traditionally, and in a noticeable exception to the rule,[14] American public opinion concerning the Arab-Israel conflict has been relatively stable, with changes occurring along consistent, long-term patterns. Indeed, as demonstrated by reactions to the war in Lebanon, erratic zigzags are both rare and short-lived. Yet their incremental attritional effect on the more stable trends can and should be assessed.[15] Thus, the study of both long-term trends and short-term developments in US public attitudes offers important insights into future courses that define "boundaries beyond which no American administration will step."[16] This point is also made by William Schneider and Seymour Martin Lipset: "Israel is fervently backed by a politically potent minority (one we estimated as about 25 percent), including a large number of non-Jews, who are prepared to punish at the ballot box those who seek to undermine the unique American-Israel relationship." This group, they argue, is "the only 'veto group' in the American electorate [that is] concerned with the Middle East...."[17]

In studying relevant dimensions of US public opinion, extensive use is made of public opinion polls. Warnings against the uncritical reading of public opinion surveys are common and appropriate. Respondents may often be influenced by such intervening variables as question wording, temporary saliency of an issue, expressed views of opinionmakers, and the like. Nevertheless, survey data can be useful in identifying long-term trends and changes over time, particularly when comparably-constructed samples and comparable question wordings are available.

Having discussed components of the human environment in

terms of public and congressional attitudes (as well as the environmental variables that help shape them), the study turns to two specific components of this environment: the American Jewish community and the Evangelical Right. Support for Israel appears to be the only mutually agreeable item on the political agenda of these strange bed-fellows. In contrast with American Jewry, with its consistent political potency and persistently pro-Israel stand, the Evangelical Right appears far less significant politically than some Israeli leaders tend to suggest. Indeed, it is the fascination of these leaders with their assumed new source of political support, rather than any objective measure of its actual relevancy, that prompted this author to offer an analysis of the phenomenon. This brief analysis focuses primarily on the most visible pro-Israel advocate within the Evangelical Right, the Moral Majority's Reverend Jerry Falwell.

Several other actors on the American political arena, with historical or potential relevance to US Middle East policies, are not discussed in this study. This is due to their relatively limited weight as either constraints on, or sources of support for, the relevant American policies during the period under discussion. These include the community of Americans of Arab descent. Their general apathy[18] and low level of political mobilization (under 3% of the 2.5 million Arab American population are politically organized; less than 30% are registered to vote[19]), intra-community divisions on questions related to the Middle East, and failure to master contemporary techniques of interest-articulation and coalition-formation, render the community ineffective. Also, the American Black population – although showing early signs of greater involvement, and in conflict with the American Jewish community over various components of the domestic agenda – has yet to reach political maturity and to assign the Middle East high priority on its list of political objectives.[20] Similarly, such traditional sources of support for Israel as the American labor unions seem to be losing some of their potency, as elite political orientations no longer determine or reflect accurately grass roots political behavior.

Two non-human components of the "operational environment"[21] affect the boundaries of presidential decisionmaking and administration conduct in areas central to the present study. First, the magnitude, relative novelty, and political relevancy to American Middle East policies of the petrodollars phenomenon make this factor particularly worthy of examination. Second, the state of the American economy is relevant in shaping investments in US strategic and general purpose forces. These in turn affect: (1) perceptions of American deterrence capabilities in global as well as Middle East regional contexts; (2) US efforts to shed the image of unreliability and impotence, considered a major hindrance to more intimate collaboration with various states in the Middle East/ Persian Gulf region; (3) Washington's ability to provide Israel with its future requirements in weapons systems, ammunition and high technologies; and (4) US capabilities to resupply Israel in an emergency.[22] More obvious, economic realities in the US should be addressed as they affect public, congressional and administration willingness and ability to appropriate funds for foreign aid programs.

Following the examination of the various dimensions of these four major components of the American domestic setting, the final section summarizes their policy implications and relevance to Israel's security and well-being in the middle and late 1980s.

Chapter 1. Public Attitudes and Israel: Changing Tide?

A. The "Turn to the Right" and Foreign/Security Policies

On March 20, 1981, in his speech to the National Conservative Action Conference (NCAC), President Reagan expressed the sentiment of leading American social conservatives that the results of the 1980 elections were the manifestation of a new wave in American politics. In his words: "Fellow citizens, fellow Conservatives, our time is now. Our moment has arrived."[1]

This statement is supported by several studies which suggest that, as early as the mid-1970s, deepening disillusionment with US-Soviet detente and increasing concern with the threat of war were two indications of an overall change in American public attitude toward foreign and defense policies.[2] By June 1978, a CBS/*New York Times* poll found that over half of the US public believed that:

- Washington should "get tough" with Moscow;[3]
- the US was "falling behind" the Soviet Union in power and influence;[4]
- the US was less important than a decade earlier;[5] and
- the US was less respected[6] than a decade earlier.

The American public's renewed support for a more assertive America that would regain its position of leadership,[7] when translated into concrete policies, led to public backing for the reinstitution of the military draft,[8] for a revitalized CIA that would take a more active role "inside other countries to try to strengthen those elements that serve the interests of the US and to weaken those forces that work against the interests of the US,"[9] and even for the use of American forces in specific cases of Soviet aggression[10] (see Tables I and II).

The surge of American public support for increased involvement in world affairs found its dramatic – if brief – expression in another way. By January 1980, 42% of the American public considered foreign policy to be "the most important problem facing the country." Only seven months earlier a mere 3% of the public had viewed international and foreign policy problems as

11

Table I

US PUBLIC ATTITUDE TOWARD AMERICAN RESPONSES TO CRISIS
SITUATIONS: NOVEMBER 1978[a]

	Send Troops	Do Nothing	Try To Negotiate	Refuse To Trade	Send Military Supplies	Don't Know
1. Panama closes Canal to US	58%	3%	22%	4%	2%	11%
2. Soviets invade W. Europe	54[b]	9	16	2	6	13
3. Soviets take West Berlin	48[c]	10	19	3	6	14
4. Soviets invade Japan	42[d]	13	20	3	9	13
5. Arabs cut off oil to US	36[e]	5	34	12	1	12
6. Rhodesia invaded by Cuban troops supplied by Soviets	25	18	26	5	10	16
7. Arabs invade Israel	22	14	38	3	8	15
8. N. Korea invades S. Korea	21[f]	24	28	3	9	15
9. China invades Taiwan	20[g]	25	27	5	7	16
10. Soviets invade Yugoslavia	18[h]	26	30	5	6	17
11. Israel invades Arab states	11	19	42	5	5	18

Sources: Gallup Organization poll sponsored by the Chicago Council on Foreign
Relations (CCFR) as published simultaneously by the CCFR and in John
E. Rielly, "The American Mood: A Foreign Policy of Self-Interest,"
Foreign Policy, no. 34 (Spring 1979), p. 81.

[a]"The question reads: There has been some discussion about the circumstances
that might justify using US troops in other parts of the world....Would you
favor or oppose the use of US troops if:...[or] how far [do] you feel the US
should be willing to go?"

[b]Another poll found 62% supporting this option in 1978. William Watts,
Americans Look at Asia: A Need for Understanding (Wash., DC: Potomac
Associates, 1980), p. 48. In 1974 less than 40% supported this option. John
E. Rielly (ed.). American Public Opinion and U.S. Foreign Policy 1975
(Chicago: Council on Foreign Relations, 1975), p. 18.

[c]Up from 34% in 1974. Rielly (ed.), American Public Opinion.

[d]Watts found 50% supporting this option in 1978. Watts, Americans Look at
Asia.

[e]Up from 25% in 1974. Rielly (ed.), American Public Opinion, p. 25.

[f]Up from 14% in 1974. Ibid., p. 18.

[g]Up from 17% in 1974. Ibid.

[h]Up from 11% in 1974. Ibid.

Table II

US PUBLIC SUPPORT FOR THE USE OF US MILITARY FORCE
TO HELP DEFEND AGAINST SOVIET INVASION: 1974-1982

	1974	1976/7	1978	1979	1980	1981	1982
"Major Allies"	37%	45%	NA	54%	68%	NA	NA
Western Europe	39	NA	54%	NA	67[a]	46[b]	65
Japan	48	56	42[c]	64	74	NA	51
Yugoslavia/Poland[d]	11	13	18[e]	NA	36	23	31

Sources: If not otherwise marked: Alvin Richman, "Public Attitudes on Military Power, 1981," Public Opinion, December 1981/ January 1982.

[a]AP/NBC poll, Public Opinion, February/March 1980, p. 13.

[b]Survey by the Roper Organization as reported in John M. Benson, "The Polls: US Military Intervention," Public Opinion Quarterly, vol. 46 (Winter 1982), p. 593.

[c]See Table I, above.

[d]In 1981 and 1982 respondents were asked about Poland rather than Yugoslavia.

[e]A Gallup poll commissioned by the Chicago Council on Foreign Relations, as reported in Yediot Aharonot, March 5, 1983.

the most pressing.[11] It appears that the November 1979 seizure of American hostages in the US Embassy in Tehran and the December 1979 Soviet invasion of Afghanistan had made a dramatic – perhaps traumatic – impression upon the American public. Simmering changes were thus galvanized to produce both additional support for more assertive American policies and, by November 1980 (in concert with other determinants from the domestic context), the electoral decision in favor of Ronald Reagan.

The evidence of the impact of the Iran-Afghanistan sequence can be found in public attitudes toward each of the issues mentioned above. By January 1980 the American public supported the following:

A "get tough with Moscow" policy	– 67%[12] (up from 53% in 1978)
The enactment of the draft	– 60%[13] (up from 49% in 1979)
Carter's proposal for a Selective Service registration	– 79% (with 18% opposed)[14]
CIA covert activities abroad	– 79%[15] (up from 59% in 1978)
The use of American troops in defense of Western Europe against a Soviet attack	– 67%[16] (up from 54% in 1978)

By October 1981, however, foreign affairs had resumed their "natural place" on the list of American public concerns. Only 4% of the public considered foreign affairs as "the most important problem facing the country."[17] Thus, most of the changes became muted once the dramatic event that had triggered them no longer occupied public attention. But their cumulative effect can be detected in a more gradual yet persistent attitudinal change toward the basic prerequisites for a more assertive US national security policy. Here, the shift in attitude toward foreign/security matters yielded a more generous public, willing to finance an ambitious program for expanding military capabilities. In 1969, 8% of those polled by Gallup were in favor of increased defense spending. By April 1981, Louis Harris found 63% of Americans supporting higher expenditures (see Table III). At about the same time, according to Yankelovitz, *et al.*, 73% of those questioned felt that the US "must build upon military strength so that we are clearly No. 1, and use this strength whenever necessary for our national interests, even if other nations complain."[18] In an apparent initial approval of the Reagan administration's increased

Table III

US PUBLIC ATTITUDE TOWARD DEFENSE SPENDING: 1969-1984

Year: Attitude	'69	'71	'73	'74	'76	'77	'78	'79	'80[a]	'81	'82[b]	'83	'84
Too Much	52%	49%	46%	44%	36%	23%	16%	16%	14%	7%	15%	23%	23%
About Right	31	31	30	32	32	40	45	36	24	28	43	43	50
Too Little	8	11	13	12	22	27	32	38	49	61	39	33	24

Sources: All data except 1979, 1981, 1982, 1983, and 1984 from polls by the Gallup Organization. Data for 1969, 1974 and 1978 as quoted in John E. Rielly, "The American Mood: A Foreign Policy of Self-Interest," Foreign Policy, 34 (Spring 1979), p. 80. Data for 1971 as quoted in Public Opinion, February/March 1980, p. 12. Data for 1973, 1974 as quoted in Connie de Boer, "The Polls: Our Commitment to World War III," Public Opinion Quarterly, vol. 45, no. 1 (Spring 1981), p. 133. Data for 1977, 1979 as quoted in Richman, "Public Attitudes," p. 45. For slightly different figures but a corresponding increase in the "Too Little" category and decrease in the "Too Much" category, culminating with an even more dramatic 56:11 ratio in 1980, see National Journal's Opinion Outlook, vol. 1, no. 2 (December 8, 1980), p. 3. An even more decisive 64:6 ratio was found in February 1980 by a CBS/NYT poll. See Richman, "Public Attitudes." Richman also reports a 55% public support for the Reagan administration's "plans to increase military spending" and 13% who want even larger increases. Ibid., p. 44. For 1974, identical figures were reported by Louis Harris & Associates. See John E. Rielly (ed.), American Public Opinion and U.S. Foreign Policy 1975 (Chicago, Ill.: The Chicago Council on Foreign Relations, February 1975), p. 16. Data for 1981 from Herschel Kanter, "The Reagan Defense Program: Can It Hold Up?" Strategic Review (Spring 1982), p. 32, fn. #9. Data for December 1982, August 1983 are from ABC News/The Washington Post polls as reported in National Journal, September 3, 1983. Data for 1984: a CBS/New York Times poll, January 1984, New York Times, January 29, 1984.

[a] In January 1980 Yankelovitz et al., found the American public even more supportive of an increase in defense expenditures by a ratio of 78:15. Time, February 11, 1980. Similarly, a month later, ABC News/Harris poll, found a 71% majority sharing that view. Opinion Outlook, December 1980, p. 4.

[b] The seemingly dramatic shift in public sentiment may suggest an initial approval of the level of increase implemented by the Reagan administration. The growing recognition of the trade-off involved may account for the further change by 1983.

15

allocations for defense, by 1982 those satisfied with present levels outnumbered those advocating either increases or decreases.

This surge from the early 1970s to the early 1980s was commonly associated with the gradual evaporation of the "Vietnam syndrome." As two noted experts on American public attitudes concluded:

> By the end of 1980...the public had grown skeptical of detente and distressed by American impotence....It felt bullied by OPEC, humiliated by the Ayatollah Khomeini, tricked by Castro, out-traded by Japan and out-gunned by the Russians. By the time of the 1980 presidential elections...voters were more than ready to exorcise the ghost of Vietnam and replace it with a new posture of American assertiveness.[19]

Yet, the implied assumption that once Americans "recovered" from the war in Southeast Asia, aggressive interventionism would come to the fore was exaggerated. Even the apparent crusading spirit of the 1950s and early 1960s was not accompanied by public support for the unrestricted use of force. The Vietnam War had made the American public all the more reluctant to send American troops overseas in order to promote the "national interest." Similarly, the missionary zeal that allegedly inspired Americans in the pre-Vietnam era found little resonance in popular opinion. According to two surveys sponsored by the Chicago Council on Foreign Relations, in both 1978 and 1982 Americans ranked "Keeping up the value of the dollar," "Securing adequate supplies of energy," and "Protecting jobs of American workers" as the three most important objectives of US foreign policy (all at over 70% of the public). "Containing communism" was ranked fifth – trailing "Worldwide arms control." "Protecting weaker nations against foreign aggression" was ranked twelfth (34%). By late 1978 Americans may have "left Vietnam" but they had not "returned to containment" (see Table IV). Although Soviet conduct of recent years, particularly the invasion of Afghanistan, produced clear evidence that the pendulum was swinging back, even the dramatic events of 1979 did not trigger American belligerence. The key feature of the public mood seemed to be insecurity, not aggressiveness.[20] Indeed, as the evidence suggests, Americans grew more supportive of building military power than of applying it abroad.[21] The seeming contradiction may reflect the assumption that a military buildup enhances deterrence to the extent that

Table IV

US PUBLIC PRIORITIES IN FOREIGN POLICY GOALS FOR THE UNITED STATES:

NOVEMBER 1978; NOVEMBER 1982

	Very Important		Somewhat Important		Not Important	
	1978	1982	1978	1982	1978	1982
1. Keeping up the value of the dollar	86%	71%	8%	22%	2%	2%
2. Securing adequate supplies of energy	78	70	15	23	2	3
3. Protecting jobs of American workers	78	77	15	17	3	3
4. Worldwide arms control	64	64	23	25	5	6
5. Containing Communism	60	59	24	27	10	8
6. Combatting world hunger	59	58	31	33	5	5
7. Defending our allies' security	50	50	35	39	7	5
8. Strengthening the UN	47	48	32	32	13	13
9. Protecting interests of American business abroad	45	44	40	43	9	9
10. Promoting and defending human rights in other countries	39	43	40	42	14	9
11. Helping to improve the standard of living in less developed countries	35	35	47	50	12	11
12. Protecting weaker nations against foreign aggression	34	34	47	50	10	9
13. Helping to bring democratic forms of government to other nations	26	29	44	47	21	17

Source: Gallup Organization polls sponsored by CCFR, as published in John E. Rielly, "American Opinion: Continuity, Not Reaganism," Foreign Policy, no. 50 (Spring 1983), p. 90.

potential adversaries avoid testing America's will to use force. Thus, in addressing specific instances where the use of force was to be considered, Americans appeared to evaluate not simply whether the US should be involved in world affairs (as suggested by the traditional *internationalist vs. isolationist* dichotomy), but also the "where" and "how" of such involvement.

Six major considerations appear to influence the degree of public willingness to support the use of force on behalf of other countries:[22]

1. The importance of the threatened country to US interests;
2. The general favorable or unfavorable image of that country;
3. The imminence of the threat (i.e., potential vs. actual);
4. The source of the threat (i.e. Soviet vs. local);
5. The potential impact of US involvement;
6. The risk of a prolonged involvement ("another Vietnam").

In the early 1980s, some 15% of the American public, disposed to send US troops to defend most friendly countries, could be identified as *Hardliners.* An additional 25% were opposed to military intervention on behalf of any country in a tradition often labeled *Accommodationist.*[23] Of the others, most relevant here are those that represented the "third head of the eagle," labeled here *Selective Interventionists.* They espouse more restraint than do Hardliners and more assertiveness than do Accommodationists. They maintain that "especially discriminating selectivity should be exercised in limiting security commitments to the 'indispensable minimum,' defined for example...as Western Europe, Japan, and Israel."[24] They assign greater weight to the fourth factor suggested above – greater concern with Soviet-originated threats than with regional ones – and thus show more willingness to act when the anti-Soviet intent is the primary trigger.[25]

Confirming our earlier assertion,[26] by the early 1980s Selective Interventionists were found to be more conservative than liberal,[27] and increasingly more numerous.[28] Therefore, as far as US foreign and security policies are concerned, the American turn to the Right was a turn toward Selective Interventionism. The evidence demonstrates that this was accompanied by a slightly expanded version of the "indispensable minimum" as suggested by Holsti.[29] We shall now proceed to examine whether the fact that by the early and mid-1980s conservatives appeared even more supportive of Israel and its security policy than Jerusalem's traditional liberal constituency,[30] means that Israel is included in this minimum.

B. Public Attitudes: The Middle East

By early 1980, even in the Middle East – where recent developments and Soviet conduct seemed most threatening to vital American interests – the bounds of this renewed American interventionism were clearly demarcated once the actual use of force was considered. Americans seemed to draw a distinction between image-projection and actual deeds: when general sentiments were to be translated into concrete measures, battle cries were short-lived at most.[31] Thus, six weeks after Americans were aroused by the takeover of their embassy in Tehran, initial support for efforts to release the hostages or for retaliation against Iran began to dissipate.[32] Hawkishness was then confined only to the extreme case where "some of the American hostages...were killed." Yet, with the specific crisis over, Americans were once again willing to express support for the use of force under possible future hostage-taking situations.[33]

Nor did American public views of the use of force in order to ensure an adequate supply of oil from the Persian Gulf change markedly after the Iranian revolution and the seizure of the American hostages. Thus, in November 1979 the *Washington Post* found Americans opposed to the use of force by a ratio of 49:39. This was a mere 3% increase in support from a year earlier, a time when most Americans considered securing the supply of oil the second most important objective of US foreign policy.[34] However, following the invasion of Afghanistan and President Carter's January 1980 State of the Union address, in which he enunciated the Carter Doctrine, the findings were quite different: 64% of the American public supported the use of force, while 26% opposed it.[35] Yet this sentiment, too, was not all encompassing. By the early 1980s, even the complete cut-off of all oil sales to the United States by a regional oil-producing country was not perceived as sufficient cause for Americans to support the forceful seizure of oil fields in the boycotting country (see Table V).[36] However, if the threat were to originate not with an independent act of a regional state but with aggressive Soviet behavior, a majority of Americans justified a military response.[37]

The American public's "post-Afghanistan" willingness to empower its government to use force in the Middle East spilled over into the Arab-Israel context as well. By January 1980, 43% of Americans were willing to send troops to help Israel if invaded by

Table V

US PUBLIC ATTITUDE TOWARD SENDING TROOPS TO SEIZE OIL FIELDS

IN RETALIATION FOR A CUTOFF: FALL 1980[a]

Attitude: Country	In Favor	Opposed	Don't Know/ No Opinion
Iran	26	69	5
Iraq	18	75	7
Libya	17	76	7
Saudi Arabia	20	75	5

Source: Based on Middle East Institute survey, Fall 1980, as
          reported in Shelley Slade, "The Image of the Arab in
          America: Analysis of a Poll on American Attitudes,"
          Middle East Journal, Spring 1981, p. 156.

[a]Respondents were asked the following question: "For each of the
countries, please tell me whether, if that country were to cut
off all further sales of oil to the US, you would favor or oppose
the US sending troops to seize that country's oilfields."

20

Arab forces. However here, too, the impact of dramatic events did not produce long-term attitudinal changes. Eight months later, support for such measures declined to just under 30%; it remained so during the following two years (see Table VI).[38]

Israel, which, for a very brief period in the wake of the dramatic Camp David Accords was ranked by the vast majority of Americans polled as the second most important country in the world (!) in terms of "American vital interest there,"[39] has long enjoyed a positive image as "a friend and ally of the United States,[40] "a small, courageous, democratic nation which is trying to preserve its independence."[41] In the context of the Arab-Israel conflict, the majority of Americans questioned supported Israel's efforts to build up its armed forces since "the Arabs are determined to destroy Israel."[42] Throughout the 1970s and into the 1980s, at least three out of four Americans polled held a positive image of Israel.[43] In recent years, this general support was consistently translated into endorsements of the very generous level of aid – military and other – to Israel. For example, between 1976 and mid-1980 public support for sending arms to Israel rose from 65% to 75%[44] (see Table VII). During the same period, the majority of Americans polled felt that aid to Israel "should remain at current levels or increase."[45] When asked to choose sides in the Arab-Israel conflict, Americans were decidedly more supportive of Israel. Indeed, those polled did not demonstrate great sympathy with the Arab side (see Table VIII). Yet, over the years, support for the Arabs has gradually increased from a negligible 3% in 1970 to a much less negligible minority of over 10% in the early 1980s (with the important aberration of summer 1982.[46]) Interestingly, when support for Israel was associated with possible Arab retaliation in an oil boycott, support for Israel did not decline, but sympathy expressed for the Arab cause doubled.[47] As reflected in Table IX, with over a third to one-half of those questioned expressing no preference, throughout the 1970s and into the 1980s Israel enjoyed the steady support of the overwhelming majority of those who cared to choose sides.

It is noteworthy that both general sympathy with Israel and support for specific – often controversial – Israeli policies has been higher among the more politically attentive and better informed public. Thus, several studies have found a significant correlation between level of education and support for Israel.[48] Equally significant was the finding of majority support among

Table VI

US PUBLIC ATTITUDE TOWARD SENDING TROOPS

TO HELP DEFEND ISRAEL: 1974-82

	% Favoring Support
December 1982	30%
October 1981	28
July 1981	28
February 1981	26
August 1980	29
February 1980	35
January 1980	43
November 1978	22
July 1978	21
1976	23
1974	23

Sources: 1974, 1976, November 1978: Harris Polls, Opinion Outlook; July 1978, February 1980, February 1981, July 1981: Richman, "Public Attitudes;" January and August 1980: Newsweek, October 20, 1980; July and October 1981: The Washington Post, October 21, 1981; December 1982: John E. Rielly (ed.), American Public Opinion and US Foreign Policy 1983 (The Chicago Council on Foreign Relations, February 1983), p. 31.

Table VII

US PUBLIC ATTITUDE TOWARD ARMS

SUPPLIES TO ISRAEL: 1976-80

	Opposed	Favor
1980	15%	75%
1978	19	68
1976	23	65

Source: Louis Harris Polls, _Yediot Aharonot_, October 3, 1980.

Table VIII

IMAGES OF ARABS, ISRAELIS: FALL 1980

	Arabs	Israelis
Brave	12%	47%
Rich	69	12
Intelligent, competent[a]	17	47
Stupid	12	3
Barbaric, cruel[b]	39	7
Strong, powerful	40	32
Involved in prostitution, slavery	20	3
Religious	20	42
Backward, primitive, uncivilized[c]	24	5
Friendly[d]	5	28
Treacherous, cunning	41	11
Mistreat women	42	4
Warlike, bloodthirsty	43	7
Illiterate, uneducated	22	2
Dishonest	18	2
Persecuted, exploited	12	27

Sources: Based on findings of the Middle East Institute as reported in Shelley Slade, "The Image of the Arab in America." The 1975 figures are from a study published by The Cambridge Report, vol. 4 (Summer 1975), p. 180 as quoted in Michael W. Suleiman, "American Public Support of Middle Eastern Countries: 1939-1979," in Michael C. Hudson and Ronald G. Wolfe (eds.), The American Media and the Arabs, Center for Contemporary Arab Studies, Georgetown University (Washington, DC), 1980, p. 15.

[a] In 1975 the figures were: Arabs - 8%; Israelis - 39%.

[b] In 1975 the figures were: Arabs - 38%; Israelis - 4%.

[c] In 1975 the figures were: Arabs - 47%; Israelis - 6%.

[d] In 1975 the figures were: Arabs - 5%; Israelis - 46%.

Table IX

AMERICANS "CHOOSING SIDES" IN THE ARAB-ISRAELI CONFLICT: 1967-83

	Israel	Arab Nations	Neither/No Opinion
August 1983	48%	12%	40%
January 1983	49%	12%	39%
November 1982	39%	23%	38%
September 1982	32%	28%	40%
August 1982	52%	18%	30%
June 1982	52%	10%	38%
May 1982[a]	50%	9%	41%
November 1981[b]	49%	12%	39%
September 1981	49%	10%	41%
July 1981	49%	10%	41%
October 1980	45%	13%	42%
January 1979	40%	14%	46%
May 1978	44%	10%	46%
October 1977	46%	11%	43%
January 1975	44%	8%	48%
October (6-8) 1973	47%	6%	47%
March 1970	44%	3%	53%
February 1969	50%	5%	45%
June 1967	56%	4%	40%

(cont. on next pg.)

25

(cont. from previous page)

Sources: All but "May 1982," August 1982," and "November 1982" are based on results obtained by Gallup polls asking respondents whether they sided with Israel, the Arab Nations, Neither, or were of No Opinion. For 1967, 1979, see New York Times, July 26, 1981. For 1967, 1969, 1970, 1973, 1975, 1977, 1978, see Michael W. Suleiman, "American Public Support of Middle Eastern Countries: 1939-1979," in Michael C. Hudson and Ronald G. Wolfe (eds.), The American Media and the Arabs, Center for Contemporary Arab Studies, Georgetown University (Wash., D.C.), 1980, p. 18. For August 1983 see Yediot Aharonot, August 30, 1983. For November 1982 see American Attitudes Toward the Palestinian Question (Belmont, Mass: Institute of Arab Studies, Inc., November 1982), n.p. For October 1980, July 1981, September 1982, January 1983, see News from the Committee, American Jewish Committee's press release, February 24, 1983. For July 1981, see also Newsweek, October 4, 1982. For September 1981 and September 1982, see the Washington Post, September 26, 1982. For November 1981, see "Attitudes Concerning the American Jewish Community: The Gallup Poll, November 1981" (No author; unbound paper), The American Jewish Committee, December 1981, p. 4. For May 1982, see ADL Bulletin, June 1982, pp. 1, 12. For June 1982, see Chicago Sun Times, July 4, 1982. For August 1982, see Washington Post/ABC News poll in International Herald Tribune, August 24, 1982. For January 1983, see Los Angeles Times, February 25, 1983. For March 1983 see ABC/Washington Post poll, the Washington Post, March 9, 1983.

[a]For May 1982 the question read: "Should the US give stronger support to Israel or to the Arabs?"

[b]For November 1981 the question read: "If war broke out between Israel and the Arab nations, with whom would your sympathy lie?"

that segment of the American public – just over one-third – judged to be informed on Middle East affairs, for Israel's 1982 military involvement in Lebanon (by a 52:38%), prior to the mid-August heavy bombing of Beirut and the traumatic events of mid-September in the Palestinian camps of Sabra and Shatila. The more numerous uninformed and uninterested exhibited considerable opposition even prior to the September massacre (by a 43:28%).[49] The uninterrupted overall increase reflected in Table IX in general support for Israel during a prolonged period of tension in US-Israel relations[50] (again, all prior to the Israeli move into West Beirut) may thus be explained by the facts that (1) the uninformed public – some 60% of the population – was manifestly uninterested in the complexity of developments in Lebanon[51] and did not bother to follow news about the war; whilst (2) the high interest individuals have long proven not to be significantly affected by television,[52] drawing their information primarily from the less inflammatory, more informational printed media.

Over the years, however, the composition of this supportive public has been changing. In contrast with the reality of the early 1970s, by the mid-1980s it is conservatives, rather than liberals, and Republicans more than Democrats, that have demonstrated greater support for Israeli policies.[53] Consistent with our earlier conclusion that Selective Interventionists have grown more numerous and are mostly conservative, the activist policies of the Israeli Likud government have drawn greater support in these circles. The Israeli involvement in Lebanon is a case in point. While an overall majority of Americans questioned expressed admiration for Israel's "skill" in promoting its national interests,[54] sympathy with the Israelis on the question of Lebanon was greater among those characterized here as "Selective Interventionists." Among those who identified themselves as "Republicans," "Conservatives," and "Reagan supporters," when asked to choose sides between Israel and the PLO some 70% sympathized with Israel as compared with the lower – yet still impressive – 60% among "Democrats," "Liberals," and "Carter supporters." Conversely, the latter group expressed greater – albeit still limited – support for and sympathy with the PLO (20%) than the former (13%). When analyzed on a geographical basis, Israel was found to enjoy greater support in non-liberal areas of the West, the South and the rural US. Residents of traditionally liberal areas – the East, the big urban metropolises and their suburbs – were somewhat less sympathetic. In sum, the general move to the Right has found its expression in support for Israel as well: it is as substantial as ever; it is more to the Right[55] than ever.

This support, however, does not ensure Israeli immunity from American pressure. At least twice in recent years a sizable portion of the American public supported American threats to withhold economic and military aid from Israel "if the government of Israel should become so unbending that the chances for peace in the Middle East grow much worse."[56] The impact of dramatic events was in evidence here, too. Initial qualified approval of the June 1981 Israeli attack on Iraq's Osirak nuclear facility was translated into a 3:1 opposition to punishing Israel for having taken that action.[57] A month later, with the outrage over the reported civilian casualties caused by the bombing of PLO and DFLP headquarters in a residential section of Beirut, support turned into disapproval. It found its expression in unprecedented public demand for military sanctions, however limited, against Israel.[58] Israel's June 1982 move into Lebanon produced a seemingly more confusing contradiction in public reaction. On the one hand, as noted above, Americans exhibited an unprecedented affinity with Israel[59] (and, even more dramatically, with its prime minister, Menachem Begin[60]) as well as persistent, broad sympathy with Jerusalem's insistence on staying in Lebanon until its military and political objectives were attained. Concurrently, however, once images of the cost in civilian lives of the Israeli operation were shaped, this general approval became qualified. Americans remained sympathetic with Israel's objectives, but expressed opposition to the means employed. Once again, they supported limited punishment of Israel. Thus, for example, an early July poll concluded that:[61]

    a. "Support for Israel in the United States [was] actually ...higher than after the Camp David Accords in September 1978."

    b. "...the American public's view of Begin has soared since January [1982]. Begin got 43% favorable impressions at the start of the year; 53% in March; and 60% now."

    c. On the question "do you think the Israeli army should or should not..." the responses were:

	Should	Should Not
– "Finish the job of pushing the PLO out of Lebanon"	46%	24%
– "Hold its positions in Lebanon until the Syrians agree to leave Lebanon"	46	18
– "Stay until a strong central Lebanese government is established"	47	21
– "Remain until a buffer zone is established"	51	18
– "Get out of Lebanon right away"	31	45
– "Have attacked Lebanon to begin with"	24	50

   d. 55% said Congress should block the Reagan administra-
      tion's plan to sell 75 more F-16 fighter planes to Israel.
      Only 35% favored the sale.

The long weeks of repeated exposure to media portrayal of
civilian devastation in Lebanon – allegedly inflicted exclusively by
the indiscriminate use of Israeli force – served as a background to
the major turning point of September 1982. Two events that took
place that month challenged two premises of American public
support: (1) Israel's commitment to peace and (2) its high standard
of moral conduct. The two events were the swift and total Israeli
rejection of the Reagan Initiative of September 1, 1982 (coming, as
it were, in ironic contrast with an initial moderate Arab reaction)
and, two weeks later, the Sabra and Shatila massacre.

   It was then that the American public seemed to react. Taken less
than two weeks after that massacre – in which a unit of Lebanese
Christian Phalangist militia murdered hundreds of Palestinian
refugees in Israeli-controlled West Beirut – a Gallup poll found a
sudden and sharp decline (to an unprecedented 32%) in American
public support for Israel.[62] Americans, under the shock of early
reports, appeared to conclude that Israel bore at least some
responsibility for the massacre (81%). As noted above, they
translated this sentiment into support for limited military
sanctions.[63] Yet, as American attention turned to domestic reaction
in Israel, where outrage was accompanied by broad-based – and
successful – public demand for a thorough investigation of Israel's

role, the durability of the more basic traits in US-Israel relations was again demonstrated. Americans focused their own outrage and hostility on two individuals – Prime Minister Begin and Defense Minister Sharon[64] – rather than on Israel the state and the people. In so doing, the American public exhibited an apparent desire to punish those leaders and condemn what it considered to be their objectionable conduct while preserving the infrastructure of Israel's national security and US-Israel relations. Consequently, within a few months of the events of September 1982 and the demonstration of Israeli democracy that followed, Americans, by now privy to more accurate information about the war, seemed as supportive of Israel as ever and as unsympathethic to the Arab world as they had been prior to the 1982 war in Lebanon.[65]

Short term reactions to objectionable Israeli policies have been manifested not only in public demand or support for limited punishment, but also in changing positions on questions dear to Israel. This was reflected, for example, in the October 1981 support of 39% of those polled for the statement that "the United States should cooperate with the Arab nations to ensure an adequate oil supply even if that means lessening our ties with Israel." Although 43% disagreed, it was just several months earlier that only 26% had agreed and 61% had disagreed with the same proposition.[66] Similarly, by mid-1982, even prior to the war in Lebanon, Americans appeared less supportive of Israel's West Bank settlement policy and its military activities against the PLO presence in Lebanon than they had been a year earlier. Some 47% (compared with 44% in 1981) felt that Israeli settlements increased regional instability, and only 31% accepted that settlements contributed to Israeli security. During the same period, the percentage of those justifying Israel's raids into Lebanon declined from 49 to 43. 36% found them unjustified in mid-1982 compared with 29% a year earlier.[67]

Yet, throughout the 1970s, and into the 1980s, American anger with specific Israeli policies did not seem to have a long-term spillover effect on other dimensions of the Arab-Israeli conflict. For example, between April 1980 and November 1982 – Israel's military actions in Iraq and Lebanon notwithstanding – American public opposition to the establishment of an independent Palestinian state rose from 37% to 50%.[68] Similarly, by mid-1982 46% of those questioned rated defending Israel as more important than protecting access to oil. A year earlier, 42% had felt that way.[69]

Indeed, when asked about central issues perceived vital to Israeli security, Americans seem consistently supportive of traditional Israeli positions. The question of complete Israeli withdrawal from territories occupied in 1967 is a case in point. Between 1976 and 1980 the percentage of Americans opposed to a complete withdrawal rose from 49% to 55%, while those advocating the return of all these territories to Arab sovereignty retained the support of just under 25% of those polled.[70] Similarly, the majority of Americans expressed opposition both to the internationalization of, and return of Arab sovereignty to, East Jerusalem.[71] On the very salient issue of Israel's refusal to deal with the Palestine Liberation Organization, the US public appeared equally consistent in supporting Jerusalem's position: a steady increase in public support – from 40% in 1977 (with 21% opposed) to 65% in July 1980.[72]

However, a most important prerequisite for this broad support for Israeli positions was the continued perception of Arab intransigence. Thus, for example, in January 1978, in the aftermath of the major breakthrough in Egypt-Israel relations, less than 10% of Americans polled believed that either Israel or Egypt did not want peace. Yet, only small minorities believed that other principal actors in the Middle East political scene were interested in peaceful accommodation: Jordan – 28%; Saudi Arabia – 26%; Libya – 19%; Syria – 19%; PLO – 13%.[73] Similarly, two years later, when asked whether the leadership in various countries was "reasonable" and willing to work for a peace settlement, respondents ranked Egypt and Israel highest, with Saudi Arabia (43% considered its leadership reasonable) and Jordan (42%) the distant third and fourth. The third cluster included Syria (17%), Iran (16%) and Libya (15%).[74]

Consequently, support for continued Israeli control of occupied territories was based on the argument that "Israel is trying to keep from having to give up territory and make concessions *until* it is reasonably sure that the Arabs want to negotiate a peace settlement."[75] Sharing the non-expansionist view of Israel, by a 55:35% majority Americans rejected the statement that "in conquering a major part of Lebanon, Israel once again showed that its real aim is to take over as much Arab territory...as it can."[76] Indeed, assuming peaceful Arab designs were manifest in a willingness to conclude a peace treaty with Israel, Americans favored Israeli withdrawal from occupied territories.[77] For example, with the launching of the Israeli-Egyptian peace process, a concrete situation replaced a hypothetical one. While those supportive of the "territory for peace" formula no longer represented the majority, they remained the largest group. 40% of those questioned agreed that in return for full peace, "Israel should...withdraw its military forces and civilian settlements from the Sinai Peninsula;" 29% were opposed.[78] Moreover, once the leap from the present state of belligerency to a more secure reality was assumed, positions were *reversed* on the other major issues as well. Thus, a majority of Americans were found supportive of the following propositions:

Palestinian statehood
– The Palestinian people is homeless and deserves an independent state just like the Israelis do.[79]
Palestinian state
– Israel should yield to the establishment of an independent Palestinian state in the West Bank if she can be reasonably secure from any attack by that state.[80]
Negotiations with the PLO
– "If the PLO would recognize the right of Israel to exist...then [it] should be able to join the peace talks about the future of the West Bank."[81]

Stemming from long-held American tradition concerning the need to "talk" under all circumstances, in 1980 many Americans thought "the US should meet with the PLO."[82] Yet, the organization and its leaders were not taken to represent the majority of Palestinians; they were still considered terrorists and were not to be entrusted with the future of the West Bank. Thus, 55% of respondents to a Harris poll labeled the PLO as part of an international network of terror. The overwhelming majority of those who expressed an opinion opposed "PLO and Arafat" control over the West Bank.[83] Similarly, in mid-1982, 73% of those questioned by the Louis Harris organization classified the PLO as either "not friendly" (40%) or "an enemy" (33%) of the United States.[84] Moreover, in the wake of the mid-1982 Lebanese war, more Americans (60%) than before the war (48%) felt the PLO did not represent the Palestinians, while the opposite viewpoint retained the support of 21% of those asked.[85] In late November 1982, 56% of those who did not recognize the PLO as the official representative of the Palestinian people (55% of respondents) maintained their position even when presented with a follow-up question informing them that the PLO was recognized as such by 108 governments.[86]

C. Summary and Policy Relevancy

Alarmed by a perceived expansion of Soviet power and disappointed with the will and ability of friends and allies – particularly in the Third World – to protect western interests, by the mid-1980s the American public seemed both determined that the US should regain a respected leading position in the world, and resigned to the need to protect American interests even unilaterally. Yet, the will to become involved is broadly delimited within the Selective Interventionism that now characterizes US public attitudes toward world affairs. The administration in Washington is thus empowered to build the instruments of power, but is not provided with an automatic mandate to use them. Consequently, the turn to the Right – as defined above – presents the administration with the dilemma of being expected to produce a more assertive foreign/security policy without being authorized in advance to use force in its implementation. Restrictions on the mandate for military involvement relate to its possible scope (the extent of tolerable military involvement), duration (the span of public support) and domain (the geo-strategic definition of the "indispensable minimum" security commitments). As the precise boundaries are never spelled out in advance,[87] a careful assessment of changing public attitudes must accompany any consideration of the use of force. One thing is certain: during the past two decades the American public has demonstrated repeatedly that its support for bold stands lasts only as long as the cost is not high. When the excitement fades, emotions are overtaken by reflection and enthusiasm by impatience.

In the Middle East, too, emotions charged by dramatic events fade with equal abruptness. Neither a hypothetically beleaguered Israel nor an Arab-imposed oil embargo are accepted *in advance* as sufficient causes for resort to force. Past experience suggests that when hypothetical eventualities materialize, Americans do rally round the flag and, for a limited period of time, provide their government with popular support. Yet the evidence offers no reason to assume that the application of Selective Interventionism to the Arab-Israel arena and to the Persian Gulf is markedly different from its application elsewhere: it is neither automatic nor unlimited. It is most likely, however, when the threat originates with a Soviet-related activity rather than with an exclusively regional one.

Interestingly, even support for the use of American troops for peace-keeping purposes is not unconditional. Any doubt concerning the non-combat nature of the involvement has raised American public opposition.[88]

Short of the use of force, several other dimensions of American public attitudes toward Israel and issues affecting its security are policy-relevant and thus warrant recapitulation. The first is the broad-based and persistent unconditional support for Israel's national existence. This support has manifested itself in the popularity of pro-Israel measures undertaken by the US in the political, economic and (non-combatant) military fields.[89] Equally persistent and broad-based has been the defense of several Israeli positions: its definition of security in territorial terms; its refusal to yield on the principle of direct negotiations; the indivisibility of Jerusalem; and the need to accept the legitimacy of Israeli national existence as well as UN Security Council Resolutions 242 and 338 as prerequisites for negotiations. Yet, as documented above, American public backing for these traditional Israeli positions is qualified by two most important conditions: (1) the continued perception of an Israeli commitment to peace; and (2) Arab rejection of peaceful coexistence.[90] Once a change in Arab attitude is in evidence (as was the case with the Sadat visit to Jerusalem),[91] the American public can be expected to support demands for substantial Israeli concessions – territorial as well as political. Perceived erosion in Israel's commitment to peace will also undermine public support for basic Israeli positions.

Particular attention should be paid the phenomenon of public tolerance of American punishment of Israel when its conduct is *perceived* to counter peace efforts or US interests. Although the mandate for punishment is clearly restricted to measures that are not perceived to undermine Israeli security,[92] still this recent departure from the accepted practice of the 1970s signals the possibility of considerable freedom of action for the executive branch to apply pressure on Israel. The context may be some Israeli initiative – military, political or other – that appears to adversely affect the peace process, or active Israeli opposition to some American regional initiative – of a military (i.e., arms sale) or political nature.

In sum, four major and seemingly contradictory considerations guide American public attitudes toward the main issues in the Arab-Israeli conflict:

1. Unconditional support for Israel's national existence, manifested in generous provisions of aid – economic, military and political;

2. support for Israel's definition of security in territorial terms in the absence of convincing evidence of sincere Arab readiness for peaceful coexistence;

3. support for substantial Israeli concessions – primarily in territorial terms – once a change in Arab attitude is in evidence;

4. support for *ad hoc* punishment of Israel when its conduct is perceived to exceed its legitimate security needs (as defined by the respondent) or to threaten what are perceived as peace efforts.

While the latter consideration typifies short-term reactions, there can be little doubt but that it, too, has a cumulative effect on the other more basic characteristics of longer term attitudes.

As the third characteristic demonstrates, the existing potential for a conflict between Israel and a most sympathetic American public stems from the fact that many of Israel's supporters in the US share with its critics a basic outlook on the ultimate solution to the Arab-Israel conflict that is incompatible with present official Israeli policy. It is based on the "territories-for-peace" formula. In the absence of additional Arab "partners" for the peace process and during extended periods of relative regional tranquility, these conflicting visions are not put to the test and the coincidence of views of most American supporters and critics of Israel is not in evidence. Yet any change in this status quo should be expected to expose this reality. Moreover, the cumulative impact of repeated reminders of this basic incompatibility, resulting from events within the region or from American initiatives, cannot but produce a gradual erosion in the very broad base of support Israel has enjoyed throughout the 1970s and into the 1980s.

In the wake of the Lebanon War it appeared as though the basic determinants of US public attitudes toward Israel survived yet another test. During the preceding two years, for reasons that have to do with its own perceptions of national priorities and security requirements, Israel had undertaken initiatives that elevated the Arab-Israeli dispute to the center of public consciousness. These events served as repeated reminders of the above-discussed incompatibility between present official Israeli notions of the

35

desired outcome of the peace process and those shared by many of Israel's adversaries *and* friends in the US. It took a concrete form when on September 1, 1982 the administration presented Israel and the Arab world with a formula that spelled out the parameters of a desired settlement. Acceptable to most of those in the US who were concerned with Middle East tensions, but unacceptable to the Israeli government, the Reagan Initiative seemed to have set the stage for a potential major test of US-Israel relations.

Yet, thus far this test has not materialized. The American public has accepted the notion that with the evacuation of the Sinai, Israel did demonstrate the sincerity of its commitment to peace. Moreover, in light of the basic asymmetry between the risks involved in a settlement – where Israel is expected to yield strategically valuable territory while the Arabs are to undertake less tangible demonstrations of good will – Americans accept that the burden of proof lies with the Arab side. Consequently, it has been the failure of the Arab world to produce a negotiating partner that has kept in check the trigger for a potential major crisis in US-Israel relations. Yet, if the Arab world proves capable of satisfying the essential prerequisites for negotiations – i.e., a publicly-made, unambiguous commitment to join the Camp David process – Israel's commitment to peace will be put to the test. Any reluctance on Jerusalem's part to negotiate a settlement within the parameters set by the Reagan statement, concurrent with per- ceived Arab moderation, would undermine one of the aforemen- tioned foundations of US public support for Israel. Concurrently, continued media portrayal of the less pleasant dimensions of Israel's security policy, whether on the West Bank or in southern Lebanon, could threaten to undermine another foundation, by reinforcing questions concerning Israel's moral judgment. Finally, another demonstration of Israeli use of military power for pur- poses that exceed Americans' definition of Israel's legitimate security concerns may undermine a third. The cumulative effect of such developments may be most damaging even to the basic characteristics of the American public attitude toward Israel. It may provide an administration in Washington with both the temptation and the opportunity to try to impose its will on Israel.

Obviously, this "worst-case" eventuality is neither imminent nor inevitable. Jerusalem has repeatedly acknowledged the grow- ing relative weight of the American component in the Israeli national security equation. It seems to be aware of the important role played by the American public in affecting Washington's contribution – political, economic and military – to this equation, and alert to areas of potential vulnerability in this public's sympathies. Consequently, Israel is sensitive to the suggested impact of its own actions on the intensity and extensiveness of American public support, and may well undertake steps that can prevent erosion or, indeed, help solidify this support.

The durability of American public sympathy and support withstood the difficult tests of the early 1980s. Yet, durability should not be mistaken for invulnerability. A rupture between Israel and a most supportive American public is neither unavoidable nor imminent, but it is possible. Israel's own conduct is the most significant determinant of future attitudes.

Chapter 2. Congress and Israel:
How Reliable an Advocate?

A. The Supportive Legislature

The 1970s saw a surge in Congress' proclivity to prescribe the operational details of foreign and defense policies and their implementation.[1] New legislation established congressional prerogatives in the area of intelligence gathering and regarding presidential authority to send troops abroad, sell arms overseas or export nuclear materials. A partial list of examples where Congress attempted to formulate policy by legislation includes the Cooper-Church Amendment limiting the administration's ability to introduce troops into Laos and Thailand; the War Powers Resolution requiring congressional consent for the introduction of US troops anywhere; the Jackson Amendment qualifying an acceptable SALT agreement; Sections 116 and 502B of the Foreign Assistance Act which mandated human rights as a criteria for US aid; the 1976 Clark Amendment that banned covert assistance to any of the warring parties in Angola; the Symington Amendment that bars aid to any country that acquires nuclear weapons; the Hughes-Ryan Amendment requiring congressional notification of covert activities; the 1974 Jackson-Vanik Amendment dealing with Soviet emigration policies; and the embargo on arms transfers to Turkey.

Legislators' determination to intensify their involvement led to the emergence of a growing and increasingly competent staff that has provided Congress – particularly the Senate – with both unprecedented access to information and the ability to analyze it critically.[2] Moreover, during the 1970s Congress created new instruments – and strengthened existing ones – for the study, survey, auditing and initiation of government activities. Two new organizations were the Congressional Budget Office (established in 1974) and the Office of Technology Assessment (1972). The Congressional Research Service and the General Accounting Office (GAO) were both strengthened. Together, these four organizations have some four thousand employees.[3] Consequently, congressional efforts to influence the course of American national security policies became increasingly effective while still utilizing primarily the traditional tools of the defense and foreign aid budgets.

While hardly the dominant actor in shaping policies,[4] Congress has been far more relevant to US-Israel (as well as broader US-Middle East) relations than to most other areas of US foreign and security policies. Its involvement in this area has been unique in another respect: it has not reflected the common practice of cue taking to the same extent as in most other issue areas. Serving as a substitute for independent judgment on "normal" issues – that is, issues that are either obscure or of little political saliency – cue taking refers to legislators' tendency to vote in accord with choices made by others. These may be senior committee members, party leaders or others who are judged to be knowledgeable on the issue at hand.[5] Middle East issues, specifically those affecting Israel's well-being, have long been an important exception; they are not considered normal in terms of media and constituent attention. Hence, regarding the Middle East, even in the absence of substantive knowledge, legislators have tended to take stands in a more independent manner than has been the case with regard to most other foreign policy questions. The complexion of one's constituency and the legislator's own ideology – rather than party loyalty – have proven more significant in the formulation of positions that concern Israel.[6]

This reality has consistently produced policies more favorable to Israel than those advocated by the executive branch. Focusing on the energetic efforts of Israel's supporters in the American electorate, one critical scholar suggested the following uncomplimentary explanation for this phenomenon: "Congressmen, many of whom are relatively ignorant of the issues involved in the Arab-Israeli conflict, are often persuaded to support Israeli positions. The White House is more able to withstand such pressures."[7] This one-variable perspective underestimates the role of ideological affinity, religious/cultural undercurrents and strategic analyses which, along with constituents' behavior, have long served to explain the predominantly sympathetic attitude of the American legislature. Indeed, with varying emphasis, positions adopted by congressmen and senators seem to reflect the same four characteristics identified above as typifying attitudes among the American public:[8]

– Unconditional support for, and generous contributions toward, ensuring Israel's national existence;
– support for traditional Israeli positions within the Arab-Israel conflict – including the continued control of captured territories

– as long as the Arab world fails to produce a partner for peace;
– support for substantial Israeli concessions – territorial and political – once an Arab partner is manifestly interested in peaceful coexistence;
– support for limited punishment of Israel whenever its conduct is perceived (1) to exceed its legitimate security needs; (2) not to conform with the high standards of moral conduct attributed to it; or (3) to threaten American interests.

The potency of the first, most basic and durable of these characteristics, has been manifested consistently in the popularity of pro-Israel measures undertaken by Congress. One study found that during the first half of the 1970s such measures ordinarily "gained upwards of 80 percent of the votes in both houses."[9] This congressional involvement has been most noticeable in the area of foreign aid.[10] Congress has frequently increased assistance to Israel above the levels requested by the administration;[11] improved the terms of loans granted to Israel (both by extending repayment schedules and by insisting on lenient terms);[12] initiated its own aid programs to Israel;[13] earmarked portions of aid programs specifically for Israel;[14] and, in several instances, waived repayment of debts incurred by Israel.[15] On occasion, these congressional initiatives were undertaken despite stiff opposition from the executive branch.[16]

Although it has been most effective in utilizing foreign aid legislation, congressional involvement in the formulation of US policies regarding the Middle East has not been limited to areas within its traditional "power of the purse" control. On very few – yet most important – occasions, Congress has abandoned its general deference to the executive and taken effective initiatives that signaled its determination to prevent the administration from violating certain boundaries in its Middle East policy. This was true in 1969 when congressional reaction to the Rogers' Plan was judged at the time by practitioners to have "virtually ensured that no further pro-Arab initiatives would be undertaken" by the Nixon administration.[17] This was equally true in May 1975 during President Ford's "reassessment" of Middle East policy. Then, a letter signed by 76 senators urged the administration to be "responsive to Israel's economic and military needs," thus signaling that "continued pressure on Israel would be politically counter-productive."[18]

Another important area of congressional involvement that is

most relevant to Israel's security has been the congressional role in US arms sales. Legislators' efforts to control arms trade can be traced back at least to 1935. Yet it was only in the mid-1970s – when rising weapons sales provided an added incentive and the Vietnam War and Watergate affair weakened the presidency – that Congress managed to assert power over individual sales. This was manifested for the first time in the FY 1975 foreign aid authorization bill (PL 93-559), that required the president to report to Congress military sales valued at $25 million or more, and reserved to Congress the right to veto such proposed sales within 20 calendar days. A year later, with the introduction of certain changes in the law, the present practice was established. It requires the president to report sales valued at $14 million or more for single items and $50 million or more for packages. Following a 20-day informal notification, it provides Congress with thirty days during which both houses must pass a resolution of disapproval if a deal is to be blocked. An important exception to this rule is the provision of a presidential waiver whenever "an emergency exists which requires the proposed sale in the national interest of the United States."[19]

Significantly, these measures, too, originated with a pro-Israel intent. Indeed, at one point congressional concern with the Nixon administration's intention to sell Saudi Arabia F-4 Phantom fighter-bombers prompted Senator Gaylord Nelson (D: Wisconsin) to introduce legislation for a one-house veto over major arms sales. On June 25, 1973 the Senate, in a surprise move, adopted this proposed amendment to the FY 1974 military aid authorization bill. Several months later, the outbreak of the Yom Kippur War prompted House-Senate conferees to drop the amendment for fear that any arms sales veto might disrupt US arms supplies to Israel.[20]

President Nixon's resignation the following year was accompanied by increased congressional aggressiveness. One result was the enactment of the revised version of the Nelson amendment.[21]

While Congress has yet to veto a single administration proposal for arms sales, the veto power has proved an important instrument in restraining the executive branch when controversial deals are contemplated. Moreover, it has provided a valuable mechanism for congressional debate on the foreign and military policy implications of major sales. Indeed, on at least five occasions the potential for congressional veto has brought controversial sales to the focus of public debate. They all involved sales to Middle East countries. All but one were directly relevant to Israeli security:

- In 1975 President Ford yielded to congressional pressure and replaced Improved (mobile) HAWK anti-aircraft missiles with regular HAWK batteries in a proposed sale to Jordan.[22]
- In 1976 congressional opposition forced the Ford administration to sharply reduce the number of television-guided Maverick air-to-ground missiles to be sold to Saudi Arabia for use on F-5E combat aircraft. The Saudis were offered 650 missiles, compared with the initial offer of 1500.[23]
- In 1977 President Carter temporarily withdrew his proposed sale of seven AWACS planes to Iran. He resubmitted it, and the Senate concurred, only after Senate leaders were convinced of adequate assurances regarding the security of the AWACS.[24] The deal was eventually canceled with the overthrow of the Shah in 1979.
- In 1978 the Carter administration lumped together a package concerning the sale of advanced fighter aircraft to Israel, Egypt and Saudi Arabia. In order to secure passage, the administration pledged that Saudi Arabia would not be provided with E-3A AWACS; its F-15s would be based outside striking distance of Israel; and they would not be equipped with conformal fuel tanks, AIM-9L all aspect Sidewinder air-to-air missiles, or MER-200 bomb ejection racks.[25]
- In 1981 President Reagan proposed to sell Saudi Arabia five AWACS and other equipment including conformal fuel tanks and AIM-9L Sidewinder missiles – all in a reversal of the Carter administration commitment of three years earlier. Following an overwhelming vote of disapproval by the House (301-111) and a 54-senator cosponsored letter of disapproval, Congress came closer than ever to vetoing an administration-proposed arms sale. It was only the weight of presidential prestige that narrowly prevented the veto.[26]

Thus, during the past decade, although Congress was unable to impose a coherence of its own on the executive branch, it was influential – if not always successful – in restraining, modifying and supplementing administration policies. Its efforts were always in a pro-Israel direction.[27]

By the early and mid-1980s, this consistent pro-Israel record was not tarnished.[28] It included the overwhelming support (401 to 3) of House members on May 12, 1982 for a sense of the Congress resolution (H. Con. Res. 322) stating that if the United Nations

General Assembly "illegally" expelled or suspended Israel from either the General Assembly or specialized UN agencies, the US should withhold its contribution to the UN or suspend its own participation in the General Assembly or agency in question. The Senate had passed an identical measure (S. Con. Res. 48) on April 14, 1982. A year earlier AIPAC, the pro-Israel Washington lobby, began collecting congressional signatures on a letter opposing the sale of AWACS to Saudi Arabia. Despite the June 7 bombing of Iraq's nuclear facility, 54 senators signed that letter. In contrast, after the July 17 attack in Beirut, the National Association of Arab Americans (NAAA) set out to obtain a congressional resolution condemning Mideast violence by all parties and commending the Reagan administration's temporary suspension of the F-16 shipment to Israel. The House version (H. Con. Res. 162) attracted only seven sponsors.[29]

Yet, early signs of potential change in this solid congressional support are already detectable. They stem from the convergence of several processes, most of which have little – if anything – to do with Israel's own conduct or even with broader Middle East realities.

B. Signs of Change

Not suprisingly, changes in congressional involvement reflect earlier changes in public attitudes.[30] Thus, for example, the pattern of growing public support for increased defense spending (see Table III) found a slightly delayed expression in increased budget authorities legislated by Congress. This general observation is also supported by an examination of changes in congressional conduct on key issues in the American public debate over national security policies. On the issue of US troops in Korea, for example, in the mid-1970s the Senate, reflecting public sentiment, attempted to impose on two presidents a cutback in US overseas deployments. Yet, toward the end of the decade, following a change in public attitude, the Senate prevented a new president (Carter) from doing just that. Similarly, in the context of the Angolan civil war, the adoption of the Tunney Amendment on December 19, 1975 and, several months later, the Clark Amendment, ended both overt and covert American support to UNITA and the FNLA at a time when most Americans perceived Angola through the prism of the Vietnam experience. Congressional attitudes at the time were characterized in a study conducted by the Library of Congress:

> The Congressional response to regional tensions was shaped to a large degree by the perceived lessons of Vietnam, with a majority appearing determined to ensure that local conflicts would not lead to escalating American involvement. Sentiment seemed to run against matching Soviet involvement in areas that were outside of traditional American interest spheres, including Angola, and the Indian Ocean...[31]

But a later change in public attitude toward US involvement found its qualified and delayed congressional expression in June 1980, when Senator Jesse Helms introduced an amendment to repeal the Clark Amendment. In 1981, with little likelihood of actual American involvement, the 97th Congress concurred.

More directly relevant to the present study was the Senate's rejection, in 1973, of the US Navy's request to build an expanded facility on the Indian Ocean island of Diego Garcia. In 1975, Senator John Culver (D: Iowa) introduced an amendment to bar any construction on the island until mid-1976. In explaining his opposition, the Senator asked: "Why does the U.S. need to police the [Persian] Gulf and the Indian Ocean?" His influential colleague, Senator Mike Mansfield (D: Montana), was even more blunt: "Are we not scattered throughout the world enough?...What are our so-called vital interests in the Indian Ocean?"[32] By early 1980, however, these interests were no longer either unclear or "so-called" to the overwhelming majority of the Congress. This was reflected in the general approval of President Carter's open-ended commitment to defend the area. In his words:

> An attempt by any outside force to gain control of the Persian Gulf region will be regarded as an assault on the vital interests of the United States of America, and such an assault be repelled by any means necessary, including military force.[33]

Moreover, the majority in both Houses expressed support for the president's intention to undertake the necessary measures for implementating this doctrine.[34] These included improving America's "capability to deploy US military forces rapidly to distant areas, ...increas[ing] and strengthen[ing]...naval presence in the Indian Ocean," and making "arrangements for key naval and air facilities to be used by [US] forces in the region of northeast Africa and the Persian Gulf."[35] Moreover, for FY 1981 the Senate authorized funding for the Rapid Deployment Force – explicitly designed for Persian Gulf contingencies – at a 25% higher rate than Carter had requested. It also allocated $25 million for the improvement of facilities in Oman, though President Carter had recommended only $10 million for that purpose.

The imposition of more assertive national security policies on an initially reluctant Democratic president was a clear sign that the general move to the Right of the American public was echoed by the Congress, where Selective Interventionism was championed by many conservatives.[36] Yet, the American legislature appeared at least as restrained as its constituents in the operational manifestation of this new mood. As the aforementioned examples demonstrate, Congress has reacted much like the general public:[37] the major departure from the post-Vietnam era has been in the recognition of the need for, and the renewed willingness to finance, the development of instruments of conventional military involvement. Congress appeared willing to create the potential for the use of force, but without mandating operational deployment in advance.

The 1980 elections strengthened the trend toward an even more uniformly conservative legislature. Population shifts within the United States suggest a continuation of that trend.

The most obvious result of the 1980 elections was the complete turnover in Senate committee and subcommittee chairmanships, as the Republicans gained control for the first time in 25 years. This reality was particularly significant in light of a striking, if temporary, increase in Republican party discipline. In 1982, during President Reagan's "extended honeymoon,"[38] Senate Republicans voted the party line 81% of the time. In 1982 the average was still high – 76%. This, compared with 65% in 1980. Democrats, on the other hand, were able to muster party unity 71% of the time in 1981 and 72% in 1982 (compared with 64% in 1980).[39]

Indeed, the move to the Right should be attributed less to the changing inter-party balance and more to a shift in intra-party centers of gravity. For the Republican Party, this has manifested itself in a continuing weakening of the liberal eastern wing and a correspondingly consistent growth of the conservative southern and western flanks. Thus, of the 53 Republican senators in the 97th Congress, more than 30 held conservative positions and voted along conservative lines on economic and social as well as national security issues.[40] Supported by 15 staunchly conservative southern Democrats (see Table X), this conservative coalition demonstrated a political strength unequalled in the previous 25 years. During 1981 it won 95% of the recorded votes in which the liberal/conservative dichotomy was relevant.[41] This represented more than a 20% increase over the coalition's 1980 success rate of 72%. It marked the third consecutive year of its growing strength.[42] One manifestation of the trend was the share of conservatives holding Senate committee chairmanships. In the 97th Congress, of the 15 standing committees, nine were chaired by some of the most conservative senators. The others, moderate-to-liberal chairmen, labored to align themselves with conservative concerns. They sought cooperation with the administration and conciliation within their respective committees, for fear of losing their effectiveness and being discredited – thus ignored – in an increasingly conservative environment.[43]

The high degree of defections among Democrats was even more significant in producing a conservative coalition in the Democrat-controlled House of Representatives (see Table X). In 1981 it produced victories in 88% of the votes where conservatives functioned as a coalition.[44] Republicans, numbering 192 (vs. 243 Democrats), were 26 votes short of a majority. Yet, in 1981 only 35 Democrats voted in a consistently liberal tradition. Twenty five Democratic representatives – all from the South – supported the conservative coalition on every occasion.[45] They all won reelection in 1982.[46] They were among over 40 whose conservative record on national security and foreign policy issues, while not perfect, was sufficient to contribute to the success of the conservative coalition. Indeed, in the 97th Congress the Conservative Democratic Forum – a group of mostly southern conservatives who share few views with the majority of House Democrats – had a membership of forty-six.[47] Moreover, many of the other, younger Democrats did not demonstrate loyalty on the basis of party affiliation either. Sceptical about many traditional Democratic programs, they aggravated the Democratic leadership's difficulties in exerting control, while easing the task of Republicans supportive of their conservative president.

While the phenomenon of the relatively conservative voting pattern of southerners from both parties and the liberal tendencies of easterners[48] seems to remain a political constant, residency in the West and midwestern US proved less of a reliable predictor of voting patterns than party affiliation. In 1981 the Midwest

Table X

US CONGRESS, PARTY LINE SUPPORT[a]: 1981

Senate	Support (%)		Opposition (%)	
	1981	1982	1981	1982
Northern Democrats	76	78	15	17
Southern Democrats	60	59	34	36
Northern Republicans	79	74	16	21
Southern Republicans	88	86	8	12

House	Support (%)		Opposition (%)	
	1981	1982	1981	1982
Northern Democrats	76	79	15	11
Southern Democrats	53	56	40	35
Northern Republicans	72	67	21	23
Southern Republicans	81	78	14	15

Source: Congressional Quarterly, January 9, 1982, p. 62.

[a]"...the percentage of times the average Democrat and Republican voted with his party majority in disagreement with the other party's majority."

proved more liberal and the West more conservative when judged by its congressional representation.[49]

As noted above, this turn to the Right in both parties and in both houses may continue and intensify in future elections. As far as the House of Representatives is concerned, the 1980 report of the American Census Bureau indicated that the shift of population from the northern Frost Belt states into the Sun Belt was even greater than anticipated. Consequently, following the reapportionment of seats, and for the rest of the 1980s, seventeen additional congressmen are elected in southern and western states at the expense of northern and midwestern ones (see Table XI). As of the 98th Congress, the 12-state Eastern region lost 9 seats; the Midwest lost 8; the South gained 8 and the West gained 9 seats. The greatest loss was in the inner-city districts of the largest eastern metropolitan areas, with suburbs and exurbs enjoying the major gain in population.

The political significance of these demographic changes relates less to party affiliation and more to ideological division. Throughout the 1970s midwestern and western districts voted more Republican, and southern as well as eastern districts have been the most dependable source of Democratic votes. Yet, the most conservative districts have been concentrated in the growing South and West as well as in suburban areas, while most of the liberal ones are in the declining (in relative as well as absolute terms) North and Midwest as well as the major metropolitan areas.[50] Rather than "infect" their new neighborhoods with ideological traits imported from the old ones, newcomers, with obvious exceptions,[51] seem to adjust their political behavior to their new environment. Indeed, since 1966 the congressional districts that have experienced the largest increases in population have been among the most conservative in their voting behavior. Their conservatism has not been diluted as a result of the influx of newcomers. Concurrently, the districts that have declined or grown slowly have, for the most part, been liberal.[52]

Projections based on these historical trends indicate that northern and midwestern states which suffered a net loss of 18 House seats between 1950 and 1970 and lost another 17 in 1982, will experience the loss of some 15 additional seats during the 1990s.[53] Although in 10 of the 25 most rapidly growing districts the elected legislators were Democrats, they, too, reflected the conservative ideology of their southern and western districts.[54]

Table XI

"WINNERS" AND "LOSERS": 1982 REAPPORTIONMENT

Winners		Losers	
Florida	+ 4 seats	New York	- 5 seats
Texas	+ 3 "	Illinois	- 2 "
California	+ 2 "	Ohio	- 2 "
Arizona	+ 1 "	Pennsylvania	- 2 "
Colorado	+ 1 "	Indiana	- 1 "
Nevada	+ 1 "	Massachusetts	- 1 "
New Mexico	+ 1 "	Michigan	- 1 "
Oregon	+ 1 "	Missouri	- 1 "
Tennessee	+ 1 "	New Jersey	- 1 "
Utah	+ 1 "	South Dakota	- 1 "
Washington	+ 1 "		

Source: National Journal, May 1, 1982, p. 752.

Consequently, if present tendencies continue and conservatism is largely associated with assertiveness (or Selective Interventionism)[55] on national security issues, then the predictable shift in political power from liberal to traditionally more conservative areas portends even greater congressional support for the development of instruments of power and, possibly, even for a more visible American involvement in the protection and promotion of perceived American interests abroad. Congress can thus be expected to be less tolerant when American interests are perceived to be threatened by policies of other nations. In such cases, not only will it support countermeasures undertaken by an administration, but it is likely to take its own punitive initiatives as well.

Another relevant variable in the changing complexion of Congress is the continuing decline in the average age of the legislators. Starting in 1969, each Congress has been "younger" than its predecessor. The average age of the 435 members of the House of Representatives has fallen three years in the 20-year period 1963-1983.[56] The 97th Congress averaged 49.2 years (see Table XII). In 1982, the new (98th) House of Representatives had 80 newly elected members whose average age was 43.3.[57] In the 97th Congress there were, for the first time since World War II, eight congressmen who, when elected, had yet to celebrate their 30th birthdays. Seven of these supported foreign and security policies that were advocated by the right wing of the Republican Party, and all enjoyed the backing of large business corporations in gaining office while running against liberal incumbents.[58]

When it comes to Middle East policies, particularly to questions relevant to Israeli security, this younger Congress – unlike its older predecessors of decades past – can hardly be expected to be guided by the aggregate of forceful personal memories of Jewish suffering during the Holocaust. Nor is it moved by recollections of Israel's pioneering beginning, courageous emergence and revolutionary, yet democratic, socio-political experimentation in nation-reconstruction.

Since the 97th Congress, this new reality has been reinforced by the absence of certain powerful members of the Senate, and particularly of the Foreign Relations Committee – and their respective staff members – who consistently demonstrated sensitivity to Israel's needs. These include former chairman Frank Church (D: Idaho), former ranking minority leader on the committee Jacob Javits (R: New York), and Richard Stone (D: Florida), in

Table XII

THE 97th CONGRESS: AVERAGE AGE

	Senate	House	All Members
Both Parties	52.5	48.4	49.2
Democrats	54.1	49.5	50.2
Republicans	51.1	47.1	47.9

Source: Congressional Quarterly, January 24, 1981, p. 200.

addition to the late Henry M. Jackson (D: Washington), who was ranking minority leader on the Armed Services Committee, and the earlier departures of the late Clifford Case (R: New Jersey), and Hubert H. Humphrey (D: Minnesota). Additional senators who were less vocal yet were consistent in their support for basic Israeli positions were also no longer members of Congress. These include Birch Bayh (D: Indiana), John Culver (D: Iowa), and Warren G. Magnuson (D: Washington). Although new legislators who appear to be equally open to Israeli concerns have been elected, and they have joined a long list of veterans who returned to Congress, the cumulative impact of the departure of those mentioned above is two-dimensional: first, their seniority had accentuated their power and influence within their respective committees as well as in the Congress as a whole. Second, their successors have yet to assert themselves and demonstrate a similar will and ability for coalition-building, initiative and leadership on relevant issues. This second dimension also applies to the growing number of Jewish legislators (from 30 in the 96th Congress to 33 in the 97th to 38 in the 98th).[59] In the 97th Congress the exceptions – Jewish and non-Jewish – were the active leadership of Rudy Boschwitz (R: Minnesota), head of the Near Eastern and South Asian Affairs Subcommittee of the Senate Foreign Relations Committee, as well as Senators Alan Cranston (D: California), Robert W. Packwood (R: Oregon), and Daniel Patrick Moynihan (D: New York).

This decline in the "specific gravity" of those advocating policies favorable to Israel has been accompanied by the continued vocal advocacy by a small yet persistent group of senators and congressmen, of punitive measures in reaction to various Israeli policies. This group, however, lost some of its potency with the departure of the two House members most closely associated with a pro-PLO advocacy. Both Paul McCloskey (R: California) and Paul Findley (R: Illinois) failed in their efforts to be reelected to the 98th Congress.

This new reality does not imply an automatic decline in support for Israel; rather, it suggests potential future vulnerabilities. Indeed, 69% of newly elected representatives to the 98th Congress were found to oppose "using arms sales to Israel as a way of bringing pressure on it to negotiate with the Palestinians." This constituted an 18% increase (51% of new members of the 97th House of Representatives had expressed opposition to such measures).[60] Equally telling was the July 1983 decision by both Houses of Congress to reject the administration's request for $35 million in military aid to Jordan. This was in apparent reaction to King Hussein's decision not to enter peace negotiations with Israel, and constituted a harbinger of the likely fate of any administration attempt to obtain congressional consent for the sale of advanced military aircraft to Jordan.[61]

The changing of the guard on Capitol Hill, then, implies a corresponding change in the basis and nature of the commitment to Israel's well-being, rather than a new phase in its intensity. The new basis – more influenced by short-term reactions to Israel's own conduct than the old one – involves the perception of Israel's present, rather than historical, high standards of moral conduct, as well as of its contribution to US strategic interests.

C. Summary and Policy Relevancy

Congress, increasingly assertive and better informed, has long been particularly relevant to issues affecting Israeli security. This has been true primarily for two reasons. First, the tools utilized most effectively by Congress in influencing foreign and security policies are also the ones most crucial for US assistance – economic, military and political – to Israel. Second, the political saliency of Israel-related issues has contributed to the less-partisan approach of most legislators, thus transforming Capitol Hill into the prime area for Israel-related lobbying.

Throughout the 1970s, in its testament of aid to Israel (both economic and military), arms sales to other Middle East countries, and various American political initiatives regarding the Arab-Israel conflict, Congress exhibited an unusual deference to Israeli preferences. Indeed, pro-Israel measures were most popular on the Hill. Yet, toward the end of the decade, and even more clearly since 1980, the convergence of several changes in the complexion of Congress has produced signs of potential change in this reality.

The congressional manifestation of the general move to the Right in American politics has been slow in coming. By 1980, however, not only did the bi-partisan conservative coalition enjoy a productive year of legislative successes, but population shifts seemed to promise further enhancement of its potency throughout the 1980s. President Reagan's extended political honeymoon[62] played an important role in facilitating these victories. Its termination, and economic realities,[63] have affected the smoothness of this conservative course. Nevertheless, as long as conservatism in foreign and security matters is translated into Selective Interventionism, the American Congress should be expected to be less tolerant, and more willing to take action, when convinced that American interests are threatened.

Other major relevant changes have been the declining average age of American legislators, and the changing of the guard in terms of the retirement of a powerful group of pro-Israel congressional leaders. Both processes weakened Congress' collective sense of guilt toward the victims of the Holocaust and its admiration for Israel's pioneering beginning as dominant filters through which Israel is perceived by the American legislature.

Thus a more pragmatic, conservative and younger Congress has been dealing with Israel on the basis of two major criteria: (1) its current moral image and perceived pursuit of democratic values rather than historical legacy; and (2) its contribution to American interests. This relatively new reality finds its manifestation in the increasingly visible tendency of legislators to demand an Israeli *quid* for the American *quo*.[64] The more substantial their contribution to Israeli security has become, the more willing senators and congressmen appear to see Israel punished when its conduct does not meet their expectations; that is, when its policy does not conform with legislators' definition of Israel's own, or America's, interests, or violates the high standards of moral conduct they attribute to Israel. Moreover, in fulfilling Israel's expectations that it serve as a shield against potentially damaging administration initiatives, Congress' emerging new criteria for support are, by definition, less insulated from the attritional effect of continued tension. The task of undermining Congress' commitment to, and willingness to engage in, political battles on behalf of Israel may prove less unthinkable among those for whom the 1940s are a chapter of history than among those who have vivid personal memories of it; among those who base their support on repeated reminders of Israel's utility and moral justification, rather than among their elders who required no such proof.

By the mid-1980s the US Congress was still most sympathetic with basic Israeli national security concerns. Indeed, pro-Israel measures were still popular and no legislation judged to threaten vital Israeli interests was likely to be enacted. Yet, gradually, Congress may emerge as a less secure base of automatic support.

Moreover, its present attitude of benign neglect toward administration policies of punishing Israel could be replaced by active – if limited – hostile conduct if members are led to believe that Jerusalem is not behaving in its own or America's best interest. The concept of "Saving Israel Despite Herself" has never been fully discredited or disposed of in Washington.[65]

Chapter 3. The American Jewish Community: An Independent Variable?

A. Image vs. Reality: The Absence of Reliable Data

In 1981, reflecting the sentiment of almost one-half of the Americans who expressed their opinions on the issue of Jewish political involvement, Senator Charles Mathias (R: Maryland) argued that the "Israel lobby" often caused congressmen and senators "to act for reasons not always related...to careful reflection of the national interest."[1] Similarly, Representative Paul McClosky (R: California) gave a characteristically extreme expression to another dimension of this image when he told a group of retired naval officers: "We have got to overcome the tendency of the Jewish community in America to control the actions of Congress and force the president and the Congress not to be even-handed in the Middle East."[2]

Those expressed and implied assumptions of (1) overwhelming Jewish political power, and (2) solid American Jewish support for Israel, although accepted as truisms by many,[3] warrant careful examination. Often presented as important, even as the dominant determinant in the making of US policy vis-à-vis the Middle East, the actual scope and limitations of Jewish influence, as well as trends in Jewish attitudes toward Israel-related issues, are rarely subjected to rigorous examination. Indeed, while discussing dimensions of Jewish political involvement, noted sociologists and political scientists alike abandon the disciplinary standards that are demonstrated in their studies of non-Jewish, non-Israel-related issues. They often substitute impressionistic accounts for methodical analysis, and personal experience for objective data.

Partiality toward the subject-matter offers one explanation for this phenomenon. Equally weighty, however, and more relevant to the present study, is the shortage of reliable, comprehensive data. Although American Jewry is the largest Jewish community in history,[4] it comprises a mere 2.7% of the population of the United States.[5] Consequently, national polls rarely encompass a Jewish sample of more than 35-40 respondents, rendering generalizations unreliable and the Jewish demographic as well as political maps sketchy. Figures claiming to report distributions of and within

American Jewry as a whole often originate with statistically invalid aggregations of findings of different polls or projections from local studies, which are themselves based on small sample sizes and, at times, inadequate sampling methods. These inadequacies include the sporadic and irregular nature of such studies; the skewing of samples toward the active members of the community – particularly those involved in fund-raising activities; and the concentration of such studies within relatively small communities (under 25,000) whose characteristics may not serve as accurate reflections of larger communities.[6]

During the past four decades there have been only four studies that combine the two important features: country-wide representativeness, and a large sample size. Of these, one is outdated; one has yet to be fully explored; and two, though comprehensive, still raise questions concerning sample-validity. The first study, in 1957, is the most recent instance of a US-wide census providing a breakdown of data along religious lines.[7] Beginning with the early 1960s, when ethnic identity was substituted for religious affiliation (and as "Jewish" has since not been offered as an ethnic classification), data provided by the US Bureau of the Census has been irrelevant to the study of American Jewry.

The second, known as the National Jewish Population Study (NJPS), conducted in 1970-71, produced a wealth of information but its closely guarded findings have yet to be fully explored and interpreted.[8]

Finally, in 1982 and again in 1983, samples based on a list of distinctive Jewish names appearing in telephone directories of over forty communities, produced written responses from just over 600 of over 1600 contacted.[9] While providing a wealth of valuable data, Steven M. Cohen – the coordinator and analyst of these studies – reported that 11% of the respondents "had Christmas trees," and 11% "had no Passover Seder," suggesting that in addition to ignoring Jews without distinctive Jewish names, his studies may be slightly skewed as a result of the possible inclusion of non-Jews. On the other hand, Cohen found that "a comparison of [these surveys'] respondents with those of more sophisticated (and costly) Jewish population studies revealed only small differences. Slightly more of the present respondents are...more Israel-oriented...than the others."[10]

Clearly, when dealing with questions ranging from the very size of American Jewry to trends in its demographic characteristics, political orientations and positions on Israel-related issues, any attempt to draw conclusions encounters a shortage of sufficiently reliable and generalizable data. It is only in the wake of many future replications of the more recent Cohen studies and others of the "more sophisticated and more costly" category alluded to, that the accumulated comparable data will afford identifying long-term trends.

However, the assumed relevance of this community to the shaping of US Middle East policy, particularly as it affects Israeli security, suggests that careful analyses of the less than satisfactory data should be preferred to no analysis at all. While conclusions should be treated as suggestive and tentative, the coincidence of the little "hard" data with the abundance of "softer" evidence may justify a greater degree of confidence in the conclusive nature of the findings.

B. Determinants of Jewish Political Potency

The March 1957 Current Population Survey (CPS), conducted by the US Bureau of the Census found 5,030,000 Americans identified as Jews. That year, the *American Jewish Year Book* (AJYB) estimated American Jewry to number 220,000 more.

By 1972 the *AJYB* estimate for the previous year rose to 6,115,000. The National Jewish Population Study (NJPS) of that year found a Jewish population[11] that was smaller by 700,000.

This broad margin of uncertainty concerning the size of the American Jewish community continued throughout the 1970s. It applied equally to the community as a whole as to its major urban components. Thus, for example, the total Jewish population of greater New York had long been assumed to be well over two million, with that of New York City itself totaling 1.5 million. Yet, recent studies confirmed what some experts had argued earlier:[12] the Jewish population of greater New York was under 1.7 million; that of New York City was under one million.[13]

Employing what is believed to be better knowledge of the demographic dynamics of US Jewry and more sophisticated methods of statistical projection, present estimates of the Jewish population stand at 5,600,000.[14] Thus, its corresponding proportion in the total US population is 2.7%, down from an estimated 3.7% peak in the 1930s.[15]

Yet, when translated into political potency, these figures do not reflect the actual weight of the Jewish community in American politics. Several demographic, cultural and political variables serve as multipliers of its perceived as well as actual weight. The first, and most obvious has been the disproportional presence of Jews in states with a high number of votes in the electoral college (see Table XIII). The Jewish tendency to concentrate in the politically critical metropolitan centers of these states (e.g., greater New York — 93.2% of total New York State Jewish population; Philadelphia metropolitan area — 70% of the Pennsylvanian community; Los Angeles and Orange County, California — 71%; Boston, Massachusetts — 68%)[16] serves to accentuate the political relevancy of this demographic phenomenon.[17]

The second variable is the unusually high Jewish participation in national elections. In 1980, for example, compared with a turnout of 53% of eligible voters among the general public,[18] Jewish participation was estimated at 92%.[19]

Taken together, these two variables help explain the specific weight of American Jewry that exceeds its numerical share of the electoral body as a whole and makes its political choices a matter of considerable concern to those seeking national office.

Yet, the effect of Jewish political culture that encourages involvement has not been limited to election-day turnout. A third variable affecting the political weight of the community has been the Jewish tendency toward, as well as experience and skill in, institutionalizing its political involvement. By the early 1980s one manifestation of this reality was the existence of some 300 independent national Jewish organizations and some 230 local federations (in addition to about 5000 synagogues) that articulate Jewish group interests. Although hardly unanimous on all issues, these 500 + organizations of Jewish political involvement — much of it Israel-related — have been linked with each other in varying degrees of intensity, rendering much more effective the determination and communication of Jewish political preferences. These links account for the importance of the three most influential organizations: the National Jewish Community Relations Advisory Council (JNCRAC) which serves as an umbrella to 11 national and 108 local agencies; the Conference of Presidents of Major American Jewish Organizations, that coordinates the activities of 34 national organizations; and the American-Israel Public Affairs Committee (AIPAC), the only legally registered domestic lobbying organization on behalf of Israel.[20]

Table XIII

JEWISH ELECTORAL POWER IN SELECTED STATES: 1980

	No. of Electoral Votes	% of Jews Among Eligible Voters
California	45	3.1%
New York	41	12.1%
Pennsylvania	27	3.6%
New Jersey	17	6.0%
Florida	17	5.1%
Massachusetts	14	4.3%
Maryland	10	4.5%
Connecticut	8	3.3%

Source: Based on Edward Glick, The Triangular Connection:
America, Israel, and American Jews (London: George Allen
& Unwin, 1982), p. 105. See also Alvin Chenkin and
Maynard Miran, "Jewish Population in the United States,
1979," AJYB 1980, pp. 161-162.

A related, fourth variable has been intensive and extensive Jewish involvement in fund-raising for political causes. The 1974 post-Watergate legislation concerning campaign contributions was met initially with considerable Jewish concern. The legislation, particularly the $1000 limit on individual contributions, was assumed to undermine the relative importance of "Jewish money" as the major traditional source of funding for the Democratic Party, by constraining the more affluent and more generous Jewish contributors. In reality, however, the legislation produced the opposite result. Major donors substituted smaller donations – for primary as well as general elections, and in their own names as well as in the names of other members of their households – for the previously less numerous larger ones. In addition, their traditional importance in persuading business associates and other potential contributors to do likewise, was enhanced. Indeed, it is in the realm of prompting others, that is, in organizing fund-raising campaigns, that the new legislation assigned further importance to Jewish experience and skill. Concurrently, the increased role of the much more numerous, less affluent potential contributors,[21] produced efforts to expand the circle of both organizers and contributors. These resulted in mobilizing large numbers of the previously uninvolved, with a spillover effect to non-financial political involvement.[22] Moreover, with candidates now forced to cultivate a much broader circle of potential contributors, the value of courting the politically alert and involved Jewish community increased. Finally, and perhaps most importantly, American Jewry discovered a most potent instrument for campaign finance: Political Action Committees (PACs).

According to the Watergate-related 1974 legislation, independent Political Action Committees could make contributions of up to $5000 each to any candidate seeking federal office. Legislation in 1976 removed restrictions on the amounts of the funds raised as long as no direct link could be demonstrated between a given PAC and recipient candidates. In this context, too, the American Jewish community demonstrated its political alertness. By the 1982 congressional elections NATPAC (National PAC), the major pro-Israel PAC, in its first year of operation and with a total of $542,500 actual contributions, ranked first among ideology-promoting (that is non-corporate, non-labor, non-associational) PACs.[23] Moreover, according to the Federal Election Commission, during the same congressional campaign the combined contributions of Jewish-organized PACs, whose overhead expenses are covered from funds raised, matched the sums dispatched by Washington's largest association and labor lobbies such as the American Medical Association and United Auto Workers, whose operational costs are absorbed by the sponsoring organization.[24] These 31 Jewish PACs contributed a total of over $1.67 million. Yet these totals – both in absolute and in relative terms – still failed to reflect the full potency of these efforts. It is only when targeting is taken into account that the actual effect of Jewish PACs can be appreciated. These PACs have concentrated both "defensive" and "offensive" money – that is, funds contributed in support of an incumbent or in an effort to unseat one respectively – almost exclusively on congressional races that affect the complexion of committees and subcommittees that determine future aid to Israel. Thus, special emphasis has been given the Senate and House Foreign Affairs committees and their Foreign Operations subcommittees.[25]

A case in point was the 1982 race for the House seat from Illinois' twentieth district. Otherwise irrelevant to Jewish concerns, this contest in a district with less than 2000 eligible Jewish voters, attracted over $104,000 from all 31 Jewish PACs. The money supported the successful first attempt by Richard Dubin, a (non-Jewish) local lawyer, to unseat Rep. Paul Findley, a ranking Republican on the Europe and Middle East subcommittee of the House Foreign Affairs Committee, and a man long accused of tilting toward the Arab side, particularly in favor of the PLO, in the Arab-Israel context.[26]

The Jewish PACs' involvement in the Dubin vs. Findley race illustrated yet another dimension of their political significance. In their care to comply with the legal requirements of avoiding direct links between donor and recipient, these voluntary organizations prefer involvement in out-of-state races. In so doing they also serve to substitute for the absence of a Jewish voting presence at the polls in districts with little or no Jewish population. These PACs, organized in areas of high Jewish concentration and affecting races with far less Jewish visibility, seek to increase Jewish relevancy in the latter. In the words of the chairman of one Jewish PAC: "There are enough people locally who do enough for their constituency. We look for areas that have less Jewish visibility than others, places where there are fewer Jews."[27]

Consequently, this fourth variable of Jewish involvement in financing political campaigns serves both as an independent multiplier for the community's political potency and as a compensatory factor for shortfalls in Jewish voting-presence stemming from the first characteristic: the tendency to concentrate in relatively large numbers within a few districts of several select states.

At the other end of the electoral process, a recent phenomenon serving as a fifth multiplier of Jewish political influence has been the increasing willingness of Jews to run for office and their growing success in being elected. As recently as the late '60s Stephen Isaacs, in his *Jews and American Politics,* concluded that there was "an impression among many American Jews that a Jew just [could not] make it in politics; in effect they censor[ed] themselves out of even trying for elected office."[28] Since then, the political maturity of the increasingly American-born Jewish community[29] has produced a remarkable change in that reality. Jewish representation in Congress grew from 2 senators and 11 congressmen at the time of Isaac's writing to 8 senators and 31 congressmen by 1982. These figures are particularly impressive as they constitute a Jewish representation that is almost three times the community's numerical share in the population.

Yet here, too, numbers alone do not reflect fully the political potency of the group. Although not organized as a formal caucus and rarely unanimous on an issue, cooperation and targeting have served to enhance the group's relevancy to decisions affecting Israel.[30] Thus, for example, in the 98th Congress, of a total of 38 members of the House Foreign Affairs Committee, 8 were Jewish (21%). These included Stephen J. Solarz (D: New York), who was fifth in seniority on the committee and chairman of its Asian and Pacific Affairs Subcommittee; Howard Wolpe (D: Michigan), Chairman of the African Subcommittee; and three freshmen representatives who, by the end of their first year in Congress, had already demonstrated a determination to promote the concept of the vitality of a strong Israel for American national interests: Mel Levine (D: California), member of the Near East Subcommittee; Lawrence J. Smith (D: Florida); and Howard L. Berman (D: California). Equally linked to the determination of policies vis-à-vis Israel, particularly concerning the issue of American aid, were the influential Democrat Sidney R. Yates (Illinois), a veteran of thirty years on the Appropriations Committee, and William Lehman (D: Florida), serving there since 1972. Both were members of the committee's vital Foreign Operations Subcommittee.

In the Senate, particularly relevant to Middle East-related policies were Rudy Boschwitz (R: Minnesota), Chairman of the Foreign Relations Committee's Subcommittee on Near East and South Asian Affairs; Edward Zorinsky (D: Nebraska), serving on the same committee; Carl Levin (D: Michigan), member of the Armed Services Committee, as well as Warren B. Rudman (R: New Hampshire) and Arlene Specter (R: Pennsylvania) of the Foreign Operations Subcommittee of the Senate Appropriations Committee.

A long-recognized sixth multiplier of Jewish political influence over Israel-related issues – one that affects both general Jewish political behavior and, as suggested above, that of Jewish PACs – has been the role of a candidate's record on questions affecting Israel's security and well-being in determining Jewish support. Thus, for example, the same Democratic candidate for the presidency who enjoyed the support of an estimated 70% of the Jewish vote when first seeking office, broke a 56-year record in receiving less than 50% of their vote in his race for a second term. It appears that according to many American Jews, Jimmy Carter's decisions on such issues as arm sales to Saudi Arabia and his administration's overtures to the PLO overshadowed his support for Soviet dissidents and his engineering of the historical Camp David Accords and the Egyptian-Israeli Peace Treaty. Indeed, his Middle East policies were found less popular among Jews than those of any president since Eisenhower.[31]

Documenting this single-issue dominance voting-behavior, the American Jewish Committee's 1981/2 National Survey of American Jews found 76% of the respondents in agreement with the statement that "Jews should not vote for candidates who are unfriendly to Israel." A 1983 study found 73% in concurrence.[32] Reflecting either another dimension of Israel-related issues in determining Jewish political choices or a desire to present the same phenomenon in terms more responsive to Jewish concern with being accused of dual loyalty, one observer suggested that "Israel remains the litmus test of the Jewish vote, a measure of a candidate's commitment to the moral order and the ethical aspirations that the Jewish community embraces."[33]

In sum, by the early 1980s, six characteristics of American Jewry's demography and political culture served to enhance its political potency beyond its otherwise limited numerical share of the electorate:[34]

64

1. Residential concentration in politically critical districts of states with a high number of votes in the electoral college;

2. an unusually high rate of voter-participation in national elections;

3. considerable experience, skill and sophistication in organizing political activities and articulating group interests;

4. effective fund-raising and generous financial mobilization for political causes among the affluent as well as less affluent segments of the community;

5. a growing will and ability to get elected for national office; and

6. an Israel-related, single-issue concentration of political efforts – electoral, organizational and financial.

C. Changing Jewish Political Orientation

Concurrent with the general turn to the Right in American politics,[35] American Jewry has undergone a perceptible shift in its policy advocacies as well as political affiliations.

No longer the community of immigrants of previous decades[36] – indeed, demonstrating a surprisingly hostile attitude toward recent waves of less fortunate potential newcomers[37] – members of the Jewish community had by the 1970s become increasingly concentrated in the upper ranks of the American socio-economic structure. Disproportionately "white collar," better paid and better educated,[38] its traditional advocacies of the rights of the deprived had gradually given way to more protectionist attitudes. Consequently, by the early 1980s, while still more frequently identifying themselves as liberals than the rest of society,[39] American Jews' liberalism turned more selective. They remained in the forefront of civil liberties' advocacy (e.g., they continued to support the Equal Rights Amendment, the right of declared homosexuals to teach in public schools and the obligation of the state to finance abortions). Yet they seemed less unanimous in their once solid support for affirmative action; they were decidedly opposed to quotas, and much more tolerant of the death penalty. Interestingly, on most of these issues, those commonly identified as Jewish community leaders and claiming to represent American Jewry remained more loyal to the liberal positions and ideals that typified the community in the 1960s than their constituencies (see Table XIV).

Table XIV

SOCIOPOLITICAL ORIENTATIONS: AMERICAN JEWS, JEWISH LEADERS,
NATIONAL DATA

		American Jews	Jewish Leaders	National Data
Political Views:				
Should the death penalty be abolished?	Yes	19	53.6	20
	No	72	35.0	NA
Should affirmative action be used to help disadvantaged groups?	Yes	56	58.7	66
	No	26	NA	NA
Should quotas be used to help disadvantaged groups?	Yes	20	NA	10
	No	65	73.7	NA
Should the government use stronger measures against illegal immigrants?	Yes	75	NA	NA
	No	12	NA	NA
Should the government pay for abortions?	Yes	52	71.6	40
	No	38	NA	NA
Should the Equal Rights Amendment be passed?	Yes	73	NA	45
	No	17	NA	NA
Should declared homosexuals be allowed to teach in the public schools?	Yes	67	NA	45
	No	23	NA	NA
Should the US substantially cut spending on social welfare?	Yes	33	NA	NA
	No	58	85.5	NA
Should the US substantially increase defense spending?	Yes	35	NA	NA
	No	49	73.7	NA
Political Affiliation:				
Liberal (and Radical)		34	43.8	21
Moderate		49	47.9	36
Conservative (and very Conservative)		17	6.1	43

Sources: For American Jews NSAJ, 1981;
    For American Jewish Leaders: Ha'aretz, April 10, 1983;
    For National Data: AJYB 1983, pp. 103-4.

The movement of the Democratic Party away from classical liberalism and toward state-regulated liberalism – that is, the active participation of the state via affirmative action in a manner that handicaps the more advantaged – coincided with the Jewish community's acquisition of a stake in the socio-economic status quo. This produced both the preference for "law and order" over the desire to "relieve the oppressed," as well as significant departures from Jewish voting history.[40] If in 1968 81% of Jews voted for the Democratic presidential candidate (the late Hubert H. Humphrey), by 1972, with the McGovern candidacy symbolizing a radical manifestation of the party's New Politics, only 65% did. Conversely, barely 17% of Jews voted for Richard M. Nixon in 1968, but 35% did in 1972.[41] Indeed, it was the New Politics that was primarily responsible for raising some doubt about the future of the almost instinctive Jewish tendency to vote for the Democratic Party. In the late 1960s the Jews, while no longer among the urban proletariat, still maintained a tradition of Democratic voting in the same high proportion as the poor, the blacks and the Hispanic community.[42] Yet, the ascent of the New Politics from a marginal force represented by the New Left into the official platform of the Democratic Party was perceived by many in the Jewish community as a potential threat to Jewish interests not only domestically but in foreign and security policies as well. They were particularly disappointed with the New Left's hostility toward Israel and with the combined involvement of Third-World-oriented Blacks and New Left Whites with pro-PLO policies. Having marched together in the Black Equal Rights Movement and the late 1960s anti-Vietnam campaigns, Jewish liberals, particularly the young, felt betrayed by this foreign policy agenda. And the older members of the community felt threatened by the New Left demand – and the McGovern promise – to dismantle America's military defense arrangements.

In sum, the community's own socio-economic transformation; the shifting of the Democratic Party toward state-regulated liberalism; disappointment with the attitudes toward Israel and toward national security issues among traditional allies[43] – all these combined to undermine, although not sever, the almost automatic Jewish Democratic affiliation. By 1980 these trends coincided to produce a 45% Jewish support for Jimmy Carter. While still a plurality, this was the lowest Jewish support for a Democratic presidential candidate since John W. Davis in 1924.

Ronald Reagan received 39% of the Jewish vote, the largest portion won by a Republican presidential candidate since Abraham Lincoln in 1860.[44]

As suggested above, the 1980 vote was clearly an anti-Carter demonstration. It was responsive less to his successful effort at mediating the historic Egyptian-Israeli peace treaty and more to his stubborn pursuit of avenues to incorporate the PLO in the Middle East peace process (including the racial overtones of the Andrew Young affair). However, it maintained an earlier pattern. Moreover, it reflected yet another dimension of the impact of changing alliances on Jewish political behavior. After the late 1970s, the need perceived by American Jewry to adjust to a new administration in Jerusalem that pursued policies quite different from its Labor predecessors,[45] apparently coincided with – and contributed to – the changing composition of the broad pro-Israel coalition in the American political arena.[46] Liberalism was associated with less sympathetic attitudes, while the less liberal proved more comfortable with, and supportive of, Israeli policies under the Likud government. Since Democrats were more liberal than Republicans, Israel-related issues reinforced the phenomenon of a Jewish tendency toward a less reflexive Democratic vote.[47] Thus, by the mid-1980s, although the community had not reversed its voting tradition, a Democratic candidate could no longer count on automatic support; he had to earn it. Pro-Israel policy advocacies seemed the most promising avenue.

D. American Jewry and Israel: How Solid an Advocate?

An American rabbi recently expressed his opposition both to a single-issue Jewish political orientation and to the phenomenon of Jewish PACs, with the following reasoning:

> To support candidates solely on the basis of their attitude towards Israel is inevitably counter productive, inviting a backlash....[F]or Jews to act in organized ways to provide funds to elect candidates...based solely upon their support of Israel, is to court disaster....[48]

Many in the American Jewish community, while pursuing the very policies opposed by that author, seem to share some of his concern. Their attitude reflects a perception of unease and vulnerability stemming at least partially from the fear of being accused of dual loyalty. Thus, in both early and late 1982, supportive evidence was found for the earlier conclusion of one observer that "American Jewry has yet to shed its 'siege mentality' which causes it to worry...about the resurgence of anti-Semitism...."[49] Indeed, American Jewry was apparently very much concerned about a possible increase of anti-Semitism in response to objectionable Israeli policies.[50]

These concerns coincided with more frequent public express-ions of American Jewish leadership uneasiness with and, at times, opposition to measures undertaken by Israel's Likud government within the national security issue-area.[51]

Consequently, trends – or, perhaps even a changing tide – in American Jewry's support for Israel and for specific Israeli policies and positions, warrant particular attention.

One of the possible manifestations of support for and identifica-tion with Israel has been tourism – that is, American Jewish visits to Israel. Yet, according to an early 1981 study, only 37% of America's Jews had ever visited Israel.[52] A more recent and more comprehensive study conducted jointly by El Al (Israel's airline) and Israel's Ministry of Tourism suggested even more dramatical-ly that close to 80% of American Jews had never visited Israel, while about one-third of the adult Jewish population expressed no interest in doing so in the future.[53]

Equally telling has been the recent decline in "real" – that is, inflation-adjusted – dollars in funds raised by Jewish federations throughout the US. A case in point is the dramatic contrast between a pattern of substantial annual increases in total con-tributions to the United Jewish Appeal (UJA) throughout the early 1970s, and their substantial decline since the mid-1970s – indeed, to levels below that of the late 1960s (see Figure 1). Similarly, the various central Jewish community campaigns raised in 1978 the same total raised in 1975 ($475 million) despite (or, perhaps, due to) the fact that the cumulative inflation for the four-year period was over 21%. Even the near-record contributions pledged in 1982 ($567 million), a nominal increase of 4.6% over the 1981 pledges ($542 million), represent an actual decline when the 10.4% inflation rate in 1981 is taken into consideration.[54] The total figures are still most impressive, and as 60% of funds raised make their way to Israel,[55] the contribution to the Israeli economy is substantial. Yet in "real" dollars, this contribution has been declining and, according to most analyses, will continue to decline.[56]

Figure 1

TOTAL INCOME FROM UJA:

1969-1982*

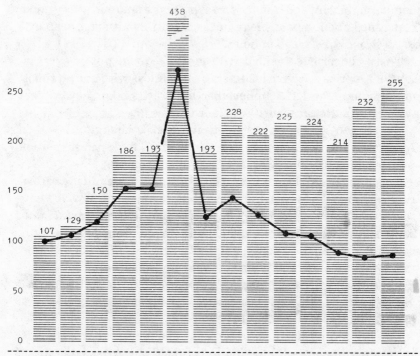

* Including Project Renewal
● Total UJA funds adjusted for inflation (CPI, 1967=100)
  Fiscal Year ended March 31.

Source: Based on <u>Report to the Trustees by the United Israel Appeal Co.,</u>
          <u>Annual Report 1982</u> (New York: UIA, 1983), p. 17.

70

On the other hand, studies of verbal expressions of concern and support for Israel have demonstrated greater stability in expressed affinity over the past few years. Thus, for example, in late 1979, 85% of American Jews polled expressed support for Israel in the Arab-Israel dispute (none chose the Arab side).[57] A geographically more limited poll of late 1980 confirmed these findings.[58] By 1981, 94% of those polled identified themselves as either "pro" or "very pro" Israel[59] at the very time that 47% claimed to have increased the depth of their support over the previous year; 41% to have retained the same level, and 11% to have become less supportive.[60] A year later, by late August 1982, 42% were found more supportive than the year before, 48% as supportive, and 10% less so.[61] Concurrently, Israel's security was ranked first in a list of Jewish concerns by most respondents (see Table XV); it was considered important by 97% of them.[62] And 71% disagreed with the suggestion that Israel's future was secure.[63]

Yet, this clear expression of overwhelming concern for and identification with Israel cannot be divorced from tourism and Israel-directed fund raising as indices of affinity with the Jewish state. Thus they are particularly important to assessments of the bilateral link between the two Jewish communities, and the findings they produce, in aggregate, are at best equivocal. More relevant to the study of the role of the Jewish community in affecting US policies vis-à-vis Israel – yet less reliably documented[64] – are assessments of Jewish advocacy within the American political system of positions favorable to Israeli security. The more unanimous the community is in its support for a given Israeli position, the more likely it is to mobilize effectively its political resources in order to try and prevent American policymakers from undermining that position.

A most important instrument in American Jewish efforts to secure US support for Israel has been the promotion of the idea of the two-dimensional link between the US and Israel: first, the cultural-ideological-moral affinity; second, Israel's potential and actual contribution to American interests. By the 1980s, the former – long shared by most Americans – was taken to require little promotion. However, in an apparent recognition of the changing prisms through which Americans view Israel,[65] Jewish efforts of recent years have increasingly emphasized the latter. Both in direct lobbying and in expressions of grass-roots sentiment, the theme of US aid to Israel being a *Metzia* (bargain)[66] has been

Table XV

JEWISH CONCERNS[a]: 1981

	Very Important		Somewhat Important		Not Important
	5	4	3	2	1
Security of Israel	69%	19%	9%	2%	1%
Antisemitism in America	66	17	13	3	1
Assimilation	39	19	22	9	11
Quality of Jewish Education	38	23	26	8	5
Soviet Jewry	33	27	26	11	4

Source: Steven M. Cohen, "The 1981-1982 National Survey of American Jews," AJYB 1983, p. 100.

[a]The question read: "How important is each of the following issues or problems confronting American Jews? Please answer the question on a scale from one (1) to five (5)."

repeatedly emphasized. Thus, for example, the most influential pro-Israel lobby organization in Washington, AIPAC, has published a series of studies meant to demonstrate, in most concrete terms, Israel's contribution to vital American interests.[67] Similarly, those seeking elected office have often labored to convince their Jewish (and non-Jewish) constituencies not only of their moral commitment to Israel, but also that they share the conviction that US aid to Israel is a sound investment whose dividends can be assessed in terms of America's own security.[68] By 1981, 93% of America's Jewry were found to hold this view.[69]

Yet, the combination of broadly-shared concern for Israeli security and overwhelming support for US political, economic and military aid to Israel has not prevented a sizable minority from supporting American sanctions when Israel's conduct was judged objectionable. This was the case, for example, in the wake of the 1981 Israeli bombing of PLO and DFLP headquarters in Beirut. During that period, although they remained as supportive of Israel as ever,[70] close to 40% (!) of American Jews expressed dissatisfaction with Israeli Prime Minister Begin's efforts for peace, and more than 50% of them felt his policies were undermining support for Israel in the United States. As to the bombing itself, while 69% justified it, 19% did not. Moreover, while 64% objected to increased American pressure on Israel to force compromise to achieve peace, an unprecedented 26% agreed.[71] Similarly, shortly after the September 1982 Sabra and Shatila massacres, a sizable minority again supported a reduction in, or freeze of, US aid, with the aim of forcing an Israeli evacuation of Lebanon.[72] Both instances followed upon a considerable period of time when at least one fourth of the community thought Israeli policies to be too hawkish;[73] this lack of unanimity in support of an Israeli position, policy or action served to immobilize the community. Indeed, neither the administration nor the Congress witnessed a wave of protest when in 1981 a freeze was imposed on aircraft delivery to Israel,[74] or when in 1982 the Reagan administration forced an Israeli withdrawal from West Beirut and the media reported that senior administration officials had recommended the imposition of sanctions.[75]

It appears that, as one scholar concluded, over two-thirds of America's Jews determine their stand on issues relevant to Israel's well-being, primarily on the basis of their perception of implications for Israeli security, rather than according to ideological commitments or religious convictions.[76] Indeed, with one exception – the insistence on Jewish sovereignty over an undivided Jerusalem[77] – many either favor substantial compromise on basic Israeli positions or qualify support for more dovish positions by conditioning it on satisfaction of basic requirements for Israeli security.

This trend – which diverges from official Israeli policy of recent years – is most clearly demonstrated in the case of American Jewry's positions on negotiations with the PLO. While the majority consistently oppose such negotiations in the absence of demonstrations of peaceful intent (most clearly so when leading questions refer bluntly to the organization's aim of destroying Israel), once evidence of peaceful intent is assumed, positions are reversed and a majority favors Israel-PLO negotiations (see Table XVI).

On the more substantial question of the future of the West Bank, while the data is equally problematic (it is both sketchy and, often, not sufficiently reliable), the relevancy of security considerations is also apparent. Table XVII, specifically the notes specifying the conditions under which options are offered, seems to support the assumption that the popularity of each option rises once assurances for Israeli security are presented as a precondition for its implementation. Most of these polls may not be comparable. Moreover, intervening events in the Middle East region or in the US itself may affect respondents' short-term perceptions and choices. Still it may prove useful to note the two polls taken during the fall of 1981, where the popularity of territorial compromise rose dramatically once such a precondition was injected into the question. Similarly, views on the question of an independent Palestinian state were markedly different between the 1980 poll – where its creation was conditional on assurances for Israel's safety – and the September 1981 one – where it was not; or between the unconditional September 1982 phrasing and the strictly security-conditional phrasing of September 1983.

Interestingly, while those identified as leaders of American Jewry seem to have a fairly clear concept of the desired solution for the West Bank as well as tactical measures that may expedite a solution,[78] the community as a whole is divided both on the desired formula and the desirability of unilateral Israeli concessions.[79] In the absence of an Arab quid pro quo, some consider such unilateral acts as a freeze on settlements to constitute appeasement.[80]

In sum, the following seem to characterize American Jewry's stands on issues involved in the Arab-Israel conflict, specifically

74

Table XVI

AMERICAN JEWRY ON NEGOTIATIONS WITH THE PLO: 1980-1983

	1980		1981		4/1983		9/1983	
	Yes	No	Yes	No	Yes	No	Yes	No
Unconditional demand for Israel to negotiate with the PLO	29%	53%	18%	74%	NA	NA	NA	NA
Demand that Israel negotiate with the PLO provided the organization recognizes it and abandons the use of terrorism	53%	34%	69%	23%	57.2%	28.3%	70%	17%

Sources and notes:

For 1980 "unconditional": Jewish Post and Opinion, September 12, 1980, referring to greater New York residents alone.

For 1980 "conditional" : Harris Poll, B'nai B'rith Messenger, October 17, 1980. See also Ha'aretz, October 3, 1980.

For 1981 "unconditional": NSAJ 1981, p. 2. The question read: "Israel is right not to agree to sit down with the PLO, because the PLO is a terrorist organization that wants to destroy Israel."

For 1981 "conditional" : Gallup poll, Newsweek, September 14, 1981, p. 12.

For 4/1983 : Ha'aretz, April 10, 1983. This poll was conducted among Jewish leaders alone.

For 9/1983 : Steven M. Cohen, "The 1983 National Survey of American Jews and Jewish Communal Leaders" (New York: The American Jewish Committee), September 1983, p. 18.

In a separate questionnaire for American leaders, 73% supported the "conditional" demand, 17% opposed it.

Table XVII

AMERICAN JEWISH OPINION ON AN ACCEPTABLE FORMULA FOR THE
FUTURE OF THE WEST BANK: 1980-1983

	Territorial Compromise		Palestinian State		Permanent Israeli Control		Autonomy
	Yes	No	Yes	No	Yes	No	
9/80	31	39	35	36			
9/81	14		9		29		32
Fall/81	41	41	28	42	42		
8/82	31	52					
9/82	45		7		19		
4/83(L)	77	12			31	48	
9/83	42	34	48	26	42	29	
9/83(L)	74	16	51	28	21	59	

Sources and notes:

9/80 : (New York City alone) Jewish Post and Opinion, September 12, 1980. The two questions referred to (1) the establishment of a Palestinian state after an overall peace is reached; and (2) return of territories save for Jerusalem if such a move were to bring peace.

9/81 : Gallup poll, Newsweek, September 14, 1981, p. 12. The "Autonomy" option was presented as "military control by Israel but civil control by the Palestinians themselves."

Fall/81 : NSAJ 1981, p. 2. The territorial compromise was conditioned on assured peace and secure borders for Israel; the Palestinian state option was presented as the only alternative to Israeli annexation (thus, the derived 42% supporting Israeli sovereignty).

8/82 : American Jewish Committee poll, Ma'ariv, September 10, 17, 1982. Territorial compromise was conditional on peace and security.

9/82 : Newsweek, October 4, 1982, p. 11. Territorial compromise was presented as a return to Jordanian sovereignty under a demilitarized regime.

4/83(L) : Steven M. Cohen & Wacher poll of American Jewish leaders, Ha'aretz, April 10, 1983 [the designation (L) refers to "Leaders"]. Territorial compromise was conditional on credible assurances for peace. A related question, suggesting an end to Israeli control over the West Bank without offering an alternative, was supported by 67% and opposed by 17%.

9/83;
9/83(L) : Steven M. Cohen, 1983, "The 1983 National Survey," p. 18. Sample confined to only five major Jewish organizations. The Palestinian state option and the territorial compromise were conditional on not positing added threats to Israel. Respondents were asked about a "Palestinian Homeland."

76

those relevant to Israeli security:

1. A deeply held and broadly shared commitment to Israel's existence, security and well-being;

2. commitment to, and mobilization on behalf of, continued and growing American economic, political and military assistance to Israel;

3. commitment to a united and Israeli Jerusalem;

4. a broadly shared perception of on-going security threats to Israel's very existence;

5. a security-centered prism through which are formed perceptions of, and positions on, specific strategic and tactical measures within the peace process, including:

   a. insistence on security guarantees prior to strategic concessions by Israel;
   b. lack of unanimity on the desired territorial outcome of the peace process;
   c. lack of unanimity on the desirability of tactical Israeli concessions prior to an Arab quid pro quo;
   d. clear division between a predominantly dovish leadership and a much divided "grass roots;"
   e. majority support for specific Israeli security measures, even if these are considered objectionable by the immediate American environment; and
   f. sizable minority support for punitive measures when Israeli actions or policies are deemed objectionable;

6. lack of effective community-wide efforts on behalf of Israel whenever a sizable minority disagrees with Israel's position; and lastly,

7. concern with the implications for American Jewry of any deterioration in US-Israel relations.

E. Signs of Change: Hard Times Ahead

By the early 1980s, three of the earlier-identified six multipliers of the political potency of American Jewry appeared to be undergoing change. If these trends continue, the implications for pro-Israel advocacies on the American political arena may be ominous. The changing multipliers are:

1. Residential concentration in politically-critical districts of states with a high number of voters in the electoral college;

2. generous fund-raising for political causes; and

3. Israel-related, single issue concentration of political efforts.

The most visible of these trends has been the changing intra-US migration pattern of American Jews. As Jews increasingly enter occupations requiring mobility; as more of them are attracted by economic and educational opportunities in non-metropolitan areas; as family ties weaken; and as fewer Jews – particularly third generation Americans – feel it necessary to live in areas of high Jewish density, Jews have migrated in increasing numbers away from the major centers of Jewish population (see Table XVIII). Even while distinct metropolitan centers of Jewish concentration remain, their relative political value is bound to drop. This is derived from the pattern of redistribution that suggests a decline in Jewish residential preserves in the politically critical central-city districts of the metropolitan centers of northeastern states. These are the states that enjoy a high number of electoral votes. Moreover, some reduction in the suburban population may also occur as Jews join the movement to non-metropolitan, smaller urban and even rural localities.[81] Although the areas of previous residence may eventually lose their centrality within the electoral system, Jewish migration may not flow into the new centers of gravity. Moreover, migration may have a deleterious effect not only on the community but on the political value of the migrant as well. This may be attributed primarily to the tendency of new migrants to be less active in their new communities than veterans, and to the fact that future migration plans tend to reduce further an individual's incentive to invest resources in such involvement.[82] The large percent of younger generation American Jews who plan to change residence upon establishing a family (see Table XIX), is bound to produce a geographically more dispersed Jewish population in the decades ahead. Consequently, this population is likely to be less potent in influencing the political process and less effective in articulating Israel-related group interests.

The continuing decline in Jewish fund-raising threatens to further undermine the political weight of the community. Shifts from business to professional occupations and from self-employment to salaried positions have been suggested as causes for reduction in the economic potential of the prospective donor as well as in his social need for status-acquisition. Both are commonly accepted as prerequisites for contributions.[83] Concurrently, several studies have concluded that "today's younger Jews are indeed less likely to contribute to organized Jewish philanthropy."[84]

Table XVIII

CHANGING AMERICAN JEWISH POPULATION BY REGION: 1930-1982

	1930	1968	1977	1979	1982
Northeast	68.3%	64.0%	59.8%	57.9%	54.3%
North Central	19.6	12.5	12.4	11.9	12.2
South	7.6	10.3	14.1	15.8	17.2
West	4.6	13.2	13.7	14.3	16.3

Sources: AJYB 1981, p. 31; AJYB 1983, p. 127. For similar findings for the years 1971 and 1979, see Gallup poll, reported in AJYB 1983, p. 121.

Table XIX

AMERICAN JEWISH MOBILITY: 1974 vs. 1965

Age Group	Different City, Same State as 1965	Different State from 1965	Planning to Move Within 5 years
20-24	28.3%	8.0%	47%
25-29	21.3	22.8	61
30-34	30.8	18.8	29
35-39	28.7	7.1	19
40-44	22.1	12.1	15-19
45-49	16.6	11.9	15-19
50-54	17.7	6.5	15-19
55-59	13.6	3.4	15-19
60-64	12.4	4.8	15-19
65-69	14.8	10.9	15-19
70-74	17.5	8.2	15-19
75-79	17.6	4.0	15-19
80+	24.6	5.2	NA

Source: Based on data from NJPS, Mobility, New York, 1974 as quoted in Sidney Goldstein, "Jews in the United States: Perspectives from Demography," AJYB 1981, pp. 39-40.

If materialized, the decline in American Jewish contributions to political campaigns may have an indirect – but potentially significant – effect on US policy vis-à-vis Israel. Candidates for federal office may be less concerned with courting the traditionally most homogenous and politically visible pro-Israel constituency. Yet, this trend may have a more immediate and direct effect on relations between American Jewry and Israel. For example, it involves the traditional channeling of some 60% of total funds raised to Israel (and Soviet Jewry-related activities), while 40% remain for the various needs of local Jewish federations. Recent cutbacks in public funds for health care facilities and other social services as imposed by the US government have affected Jewish institutions no less than other private voluntary organizations (PVOs). Together with increasing concern with anti-Semitism, declining youth awareness of Jewish identity and involvement with Jewish causes, and increasing mixed marriages, these have combined to exert greater pressures to strengthen local communities as well as their instruments for promoting greater internal cohesion.[85] Faced with the prospect of declining resources, the community is bound to intensify its debate over Israel's relative share. Yet, as one scholar has already concluded, the problem may not be confined to money: "The equilibrium that had been struck over the last three decades...has now changed.... While...Israel has been the core and American Jewry the periphery in a Zionist-Jewish ideological sense...," this may no longer be the case.[86] In the words of another Jewish leader, as pro-Israel activities have failed to prevent assimilation, have not removed the fear of anti-Semitism, have not brought the unidentified to identify with Jewish causes, but have produced an identity dilemma, the comprehensive and intensive efforts on behalf of Israel may gradually give way to greater efforts on behalf of the American-Jewish community itself.[87]

Another dilemma facing American Jewry – one that became a subject of open discussion by the early 1980s – may also contribute to less harmonious relations between a demanding Israel and a concerned American Jewish community. This involves a conflict between the two major concerns of American Jews. It is also related to an emerging perception of the implications for American Jews of Israeli policies under a Likud-led coalition. As noted above, American Jews identify Israeli security as their prime concern. Consequently, they have supported Israeli security measures (e.g., in Lebanon, on the West Bank) even when these were deemed objectionable not only by their immediate non-Jewish milieu but also by a sizable and audible minority in their own midst. Yet their very support has been interpreted in Jerusalem as encouragement for future activist policies when these very policies have been blamed by American Jewry for undermining support for Israel in the US.[88] Assuming that deterioration in US-Israel relations serves as a catalyst for anti-Semitism, and considering that anti-Semitism is their second most pressing concern (see Table XV), American Jews are faced with the incompatibility of their two most important objectives: supporting Israeli security policies on the one hand; and easing concerns for the community's own safety and well-being on the other.

The debate over Israel's relative precedence on the short list of most pressing concerns of America's Jewry has yielded a wealth of public expressions of dissent over the extent of justified political and economic efforts on its behalf. These are reinforced by a lack of unanimity in assessments of the appropriateness of the means employed by Jerusalem in pursuit of national objectives which themselves are subject to debate. While most American Jews have traditionally maintained that only those who live in Israel and face the dangers should speak out on issues affecting Israeli security and well-being, by the early 1980s an important and sizable portion of the community believed otherwise.[89] Indeed, what had been earlier but marginal expressions of dissent now turned into an unprecedented wave of protest. This climaxed with the outrage over Israel's conduct in the immediate aftermath of the Phalanges' massacre of Palestinians in Lebanon's Sabra and Shatila camps. It was triggered a few days earlier, by the swift Israeli rejection of the Reagan Plan of September 1, 1982. Indeed, the latter not only produced considerable debate inside the community but also a loud voice of support, however qualified, for the American president's proposal. Tom Dine, director of the leading pro-Israel lobby in Washington, AIPAC, and Kenneth J. Bialkin, national chairman of the Anti-Defamation League of B'nai B'rith, were among the leading supportive voices.[90]

Toward the mid-1980s the discrepancy between more hawkish grass roots, largely supportive of activist Israeli policies, and an outspoken, critical and more dovish leadership did not seem to be narrowing. Equally relevant, the ratio between supporters and dissenters in the community as a whole still predominantly favored the former. Yet, the entire web of conflicting interests and continuing dilemmas of America's Jews; the possible implications of "voting with their feet" by the overwhelming majority that has never visited the country and the sizable minority that has no interest in doing so; the early signs of possible decline in financial mobilization on behalf of Israel; and mounting evidence of changing American Jewish demography – all seem to point in the same direction, and may converge in time. If not carefully monitored and addressed, the early 1990s may present Israel with the simultaneous consequences of both a politically less potent and a less supportive American Jewry. While demographic trends in America are obviously beyond its control, Israel can affect the willingness to mobilize on its behalf. Recognition of the major determinants of American Jewry's collective will is the obvious prerequisite.

F. Summary and Policy Relevancy

As suggested by the discussion above, any attempt to assess the direction and impact of inputs from American Jewry to the shaping of US policies that are relevant to Israeli security must be undertaken within a clearly defined time-frame. This is primarily due to the fact that of the six multipliers of the community's political influence, five have been undergoing changes that are bound to alter the weight of the Jewish factor in American politics. However, these changes are neither unidirectional nor totally insensitive to intervening variables as to point to obvious short-to-medium term changes. Indeed, it appears that they are sufficiently slow in maturing to suggest that present realities are likely to continue to characterize the community's involvement during much of the 1980s. Finally, Israeli policies can affect both the direction and pace of some of these trends.

Exceptionally high degrees of voter participation, and political mobilization in general, continue to characterize Jewish involvement. Moreover, the recent phenomenon of Jewish willingness to be elected and success in doing so reinforce this variable. The long term persistence of these multipliers of the specific weight of Jews in American politics, contrasts with other determinants, where early signs of change, if not reversed, may converge to produce a less potent Jewish community within a decade or two. These include such demographic trends as changing occupational and (related) residential characteristics that threaten to yield a more dispersed community with a declining aggregated dispensable income and disintegrating links to metropolitan communal centers. Consequently, the potential coincidence of less significant Jewish electoral visibility in the metropolitan centers of politically critical states on the one hand, with a possibly reduced share in the total sums raised for political campaigns on the other, may undermine politicians' sensitivity and responsiveness to Jewish preferences and concerns.

A related consequence of these trends may well be a sharpened debate over Israel's share in funds raised in the US. With a shrinking pie, a likely reduced government contribution, and growing needs for more numerous, less concentrated centers of Jewish services and communal activities – political or otherwise – the rationale for providing Israel with 60% of funds collected will be subject to considerable challenge.

Clearly, Israeli policies that run counter to American Jewish thinking can hasten this process. Since such policies aggravate concern for the community's own well-being, they may also undermine its largely unidimensional political behavior, where implications for Israel have served as a powerful determinant of political choices. The perceived correlation between lack of harmony in US-Israel relations on the one hand and active anti-Semitism in the US on the other should be understood as an important prism through which Jewish support for Israeli needs is filtered. Finally, in the immediate future, such policies increase the frequency of virtual community paralysis whenever large minorities within American Jewry disapprove of Israel's conduct. Concurrently, however, and of relevance both to long-term trends and short-term developments, Israeli policies can ease long-term pressures for a less exclusive and visible pro-Israel role for American Jewry – both on the individual and communal levels. An emphasis on coordination and greater cooperation with Washington will reduce friction between the two countries, and thus also remove short-term obstacles to effective community efforts on behalf of Israel.

Obviously this may prove particularly difficult once US-Israel relations focus on the future of the West Bank, Gaza Strip, Golan Heights and their inhabitants. Party to Israel's perceptions of on-going threats emanating from a largely hostile Arab neighborhood, the community accepts the basic logic of Israeli security concerns. Moreover, America's Jewry is convinced that only a strong Israel can serve as an incentive for the pursuit of peaceful accommodation by its adversaries. And it is supportive of Israel's national consensus on the question of the indivisibility of, and continued Israeli sovereignty over Jerusalem. But a plurality of American Jewry questions the wisdom of present Israeli refusal to make tactical and reversible unilateral concessions (e.g., a temporary freeze on settlements even prior to the advent of convincing evidence of Arab peaceful intent). Moreover, the community does not support maximalist Israeli demands on the territorial and political dimensions of a possible settlement. Indeed, it seems to accept the formula of territories-for-peace that is shared by most Americans concerned with the issue.[91] The majority in the community rejects the concept that within the context of a peaceful accommodation, continued unrestricted control over these territories is an indispensable element of the overall equation of Israeli security. Many American Jews argue for tactical measures that may facilitate negotiations leading to the termination of at least civilian Israeli control over much of these territories, and a plurality within the community assumes that a withdrawal for peace may provide greater security than would continued unlimited control that is judged to rule out accommodation.

Consequently, American Jews mobilize resources and labor tirelessly to perpetuate and expand US economic and military aid to Israel in order to enable Israel to maintain a reasonable standard of living while providing what Jerusalem defines as an adequate level of security. Concurrently, however, they seem paralyzed when called upon by Jerusalem to lobby against American initiatives that call for compromises by Arabs and Israelis alike.

In sum there is little doubt that American Jewish support for Israel is firm. It will remain so at least for the duration of the 1980s. Yet, in the longer term, its effectiveness, comprehensiveness and durability should not be taken for granted. It cannot be expected to manifest itself when the community is united in criticizing Israeli conduct or when it is divided in assessing Israeli needs and desirable US responses. As demographic trends continue to reshape the community, by the end of the decade its political weight may show early signs of a gradual decline. It is at that time, even more critically than at present, that the centrality of Israel-oriented involvement and its effectiveness will depend on

Israel's sensitivity and ability to nourish consensus among American Jews on issues dear to Jerusalem.

Israel's success in doing so will depend on its clear recognition of the characteristics of Israel-related Jewish political involvement, most notably the following:

1. Lack of unanimity on the territorial outcome of the peace process;

2. lack of unanimity on the desirability of tactical Israeli concessions;

3. lack of effective community-wide efforts on behalf of Israel whenever a sizable minority disagrees with Israel's position; and

4. concern with the implications for American Jewry of any deterioration in US-Israel relations.

Chapter 4. The Moral Majority and Israel:
A Footnote?

A. Falwell et al: An Israeli Fascination

At his first news conference as president-elect, Ronald Reagan was asked about the likely influence of the Moral Majority inside the White House. His reply was: "I am not going to separate myself from the people who elected us and sent us there."[1] Earlier, Reagan had been the only presidential candidate to speak before the National Affairs Briefing, a two-day political-religious summit meeting held in Dallas, Texas, in August 1980 where the Moral Majority played a leading role in formulating an evangelical agenda for the 1980s. Cognizant of the fact that those gathered in Dallas were prevented by law from publicly endorsing his candidacy,[2] candidate Reagan announced his endorsement of them and their deeds.[3]

Rightly or wrongly, the Moral Majority, along with other individuals and organizations that form the New Right,[4] viewed the results of the 1980 elections as a confirmation of their credibility as a force in American politics. Claiming growing public and financial support, they purport to epitomize the current national spirit and to have identified the real issues: "Social...reformation, tax cuts, less government, a stronger military force and a renewal of American patriotism."[5] In their view, though isolated on the political fringe during the 1960s and 1970s, by the early 1980s "most of the New Right positions are in the mainstream of the country."[6] Moreover, New Right organizations like the National Conservative Political Action Committee (NCPAC) claim to have played an important role in unseating Liberal candidates and mobilizing support for Conservative ones during the 1980 presidential and congressional election campaigns.[7] The Moral Majority alone claims responsibility for over 2.5 million first-time voters and believes it was "instrumental in persuading 10 million persons attuned to [its] philosophy to get out and vote."[8] A less specific but equally significant weight was attributed to New Right involvement by several opinion-research specialists. NCPAC and the Moral Majority in particular were found to have "set the agenda"[9] especially in the Bible Belt states where they had fertile soil for their preaching.[10]

Appreciation of the New Right's political weight was apparently not limited to American politicians and the movement's own leadership. For example, on November 1, 1980, in an evening commemorating Ze'ev Jabotinsky – founder of Revisionist Zionism – a fundamentalist, evangelical Christian religious leader was honored with the Jabotinsky Medal. The recipient was Rev. Jerry Falwell, spiritual leader of the Thomas Road Baptist Church in Lynchburg, Virginia, and president of Moral Majority, Inc. It was Israel's Prime Minister Menahem Begin who had selected the recipient and who awarded him the medal. Acknowledging Mr. Falwell's perceived weight in American politics, Mr. Begin was conveying Israel's gratitude for the reverend's leadership in pro-Israel lobbying in the US. Several times prior to the award ceremony as well as after the event, the Israeli prime minister called upon Falwell in the context of dramatic developments in the Middle East. On each occasion, the reverend was asked to mobilize American public opinion in order to neutralize anti-Israel sentiment in the media, public, Congress, or administration. Each time Falwell appeared delighted with the approach and eager to comply. He initiated a series of public statements in support of a given Israeli position and urged members of his own organization, as well as of many affiliates, to echo these messages.

A case in point was the June 1981 Israeli raid on Iraq's Osirak nuclear reactor. In response to a highly publicized phone call from Prime Minister Begin, Falwell gave a sermon on behalf of Israel from his "electronic pulpit" in Lynchburg, Virginia, asking the many thousands of other Moral Majority preachers to do likewise. The response was immediate: in churches, religious networks, radio shows and publications across the US the message went out that the raid was justified; God wanted Americans to support Israeli actions undertaken for self defense.[11] A similar instance involved the war in Lebanon. In late June 1982 the Moral Majority's vice president for communications visited the region. Upon returning to the US, he denied allegations of widespread destruction and indiscriminate bombing and reported "a narrow strip of destruction...confined to areas of PLO concentration and/or ammunition storage areas." Moreover, he blamed "the PLO and their Communist suppliers" for having "deliberately placed" weapon and ammunition dumps "in areas of high civilian concentration." He recommended that "those who have been silent or refused to twist arms to end the terrorism spawned by the

Soviet-backed PLO should have the decency to do the same now that Israel has justifiably sought to bring an end to the matter."[12]

The same sentiment was expressed throughout the war by Falwell himself as well as by hundreds of other religious leaders within the Falwell organization and elsewhere in the Evangelical Right. They called upon their government "to work in close cooperation with Israel," whom they considered America's "most dependable ally in the Middle East."[13] In fact, they have often proven more enthusiastic supporters of activist policies pursued by the Begin government than many Jewish leaders. Furthermore, they advocated principles for an Arab-Israel peace settlement that closely approximated Israel's most ambitious demands. These included Israeli sovereignty over Jerusalem in its entirety as well as over all other territories occupied by Israel in 1967. They saw no justification for Israeli territorial concessions in the context of the Arab-Israel peace process.[14]

Falwell's outlook is based primarily on fundamentalist (i.e., literal interpretation of the Scriptures) religious beliefs, coupled with global as well as domestic political considerations. In his own words, "from...religious, moral and strategic perspectives, Israel supremely represents our values and hopes for security and peace in the Middle East."[15] Indeed, support for Israel has been featured prominently in his organization's list of nine political objectives.[16] The organization has consistently called upon the US to "stand firm in support of Israel." In a typical editorial under that very title, it expressed its related positions on the PLO, European peace initiatives, the Syrian-Lebanese situation, and the Soviet dimension of the Arab-Israel conflict:

> There can be no negotiating with the murderers of women and children and that is what the facts prove the PLO to be. They are funded and trained by enemies of the U.S. and there can be no question that the Soviet Union is the dominant force behind the efforts of the PLO to destroy Israel, Lebanon, and to take control of the oil in the Middle East.
>
> Now, European leaders are joining in an orchestrated effort ...to suggest inviting these terrorists to come to the negotiating table as an honorable and respectable party in the peace effort. Americans must never give respectability to murderers and terrorists by doing such a thing....
>
> Syria is the real monster in the Middle East. The Soviet Union is using Syria to ultimately take control of the Middle East.

Likewise, the PLO is nothing more than a tool of Brezhnev.

As European leaders now begin their parade to the White House, our President and his advisors need the support and encouragement of all Americans to take a stand for the State of Israel.[17]

The Evangelical Right's close link with Israel emerged after 1977. Long alienated by the secular, socialist and liberal inclinations of Israeli Labor leaders, the Evangelical Right found in Menahem Begin a new kind of Israeli leader. Seemingly deeply religious, militarily activist, economically conservative and fiercely patriotic, Begin appeared to uphold values supported by America's religious rightists in their own country. In turn Israeli officials – first and foremost Menahem Begin himself – were fascinated with this newly found source of political support, and showed unusual deference to the Moral Majority. On the other hand the organized American Jewish community, aware of the irreconcilability of the Evangelicals' domestic agenda[18] with its own, has demonstrated considerable uneasiness with this phenomenon and uncertainty regarding the proper course to pursue. Indeed, bruised by the evangelical and secular Right's successes in the 1980 elections, American liberals – Israel's traditional source of political support – began to organize a counteroffensive.[19] In view of these contradictions, this relatively new actor on the American political scene warrants a closer examination with the primary objective of assessing its significance to the formulation of American policies relevant to Israel's security.

The Moral Majority Inc. was founded in June 1979 to serve as the political arm of Rev. Jerry Falwell's allegedly apolitical religious infrastructure. This infrastructure had included a television program seen on 385 stations and reaching an estimated 21 million viewers; 30-minute radio programs broadcast by 310 stations five days a week; and Falwell's own Thomas Road Baptist Church, said to be the second largest church in the US. In 1971 this church's revenues were $1 million annually. By 1975 they had climbed to $1 million per month. In 1978 its revenues totaled $32.5 million, and in 1980 they exceeded $56 million.[20]

In early 1980 the Moral Majority's political network added a new enterprise, the monthly *The Moral Majority Report,* a newsletter that claimed a circulation of close to half a million within six months of publication of its first issue.

By August 1980 there was a chapter of the organization in every

state of the union. It was then that Falwell, along with other –
mostly Baptist – groups, gathered at the aforementioned Religious
Roundtable-sponsored National Affairs Briefing to announce a
political agenda for the United States in the 1980s. There, too, a
seminar of some 300 "professionals" adapted contemporary
tactics for political activism to the Evangelicals' unique media
instruments and church networks. They set out to amend the
American Constitution to ban abortion and permit voluntary
prayer in schools; to prevent adoption of the Equal Rights
Amendment to the Constitution; to oppose National Health Insur-
ance; to impose stiffer penalties for pornography and drug abuse;
and to promote US military superiority.

Israel's role, as America's "only reliable Middle East ally" was
featured prominently within this last political objective. Thus, the
preachers' advocacy of an activist, anti-communist American role
in world affairs, and Israel's perceived function as a dependable
barrier to communist expansionism in the Middle East, coincided
with the religiously-based commitment to the Jewish state. Yet
this singularly narrow "support for Israel and the Jews" has taken
on a life of its own; it has come to be advocated as a national
objective independent of the broader context of Evangelical
preferences within the foreign policy agenda. In Rev. Falwell's
words: "God deals with nations as they deal with Israel."[21]
Elsewhere he was quoted as saying: "God has raised up America in
these last days for the cause of world evangelism and for the
protection of his people, the Jews. I don't think America has any
other right or reason for existence than those two purposes."[22]
Moreover, the Evangelical Right considers the revival of Jewish
statehood the greatest event of modern history, a confirmation of
its interpretation of the Scriptures. In the State of Israel it sees
incontrovertible evidence that biblical prophecies are coming
true. Many of the movement's leaders attribute much of the growth
of evangelism in the US during the past 30 years to their ability to
present the reality of the State of Israel as evidence for their truth.[23]

Consequently, in addition to adopting the pro-Israel positions,
the Moral Majority and its associates have attempted to block
specific American policies judged threatening to Israel's well-
being, and have undertaken pro-Israel campaigns. Thus, for
example, some 30 church groups organized campaigns in all 435
congressional districts against the AWACS deal for Saudi Arabia.[24]
Others organized a boycott of all Mobil Oil products in protest

against the company's alleged use of customers' money in its lobbying on behalf of the Saudi arms deal.[25] The Moral Majority itself undertook to oppose the proposed Improved HAWK SAM sale to Jordan.[26] Concurrently, a campaign to encourage tourism to Israel was launched, involving both multimedia approaches and personal example set by the movement's leadership.[27] Its purpose, according to Ronald S. Godwin, Vice-President of the Moral Majority, was "to transform as many concerned American citizens into well-informed educated friends of Israel as possible."[28]

B. A Political Power Base, or a Media Event?

By the mid-1980s, however, it had become evident that earlier assumptions concerning the political potency of the Moral Majority (or of the New Right, for that matter) were exaggerated. While the organization proved capable of affecting public debates, including popular sentiment vis-à-vis Israel, it failed to live up to its own claims as well as to others' expectations, in affecting specific policies (e.g., the AWACS deal);[29] in influencing White House appointments;[30] and even in the area of its assumed expertise – negative political campaigning.[31]

Various polls taken in 1980 found that 20% of Americans – about 30 million voters – met all three criteria which qualified them as the natural constituency of the Evangelical Right: they were (1) orthodox ("fundamentalist"), (2) "conversionalist" and (3) "born again." Another 21 million voters met the definition of "born again" alone.[32] Several polls and media surveys found 10 to 15 million Americans to be regular viewers of evangelical programs and as many as 100 million to qualify as a once-a-week audience.[33]

Yet this sizable portion of the American electorate has not been mobilized into either broad based support for the movement's general economic and political positions or into electoral accomplishments. In mid-1981 about half of the American public had still not heard of the Moral Majority. Of the other half, 43% disapproved of its positions on most issues; 37% said they approved and the rest had no opinion.[34] But even those expressing approval appeared to have little knowledge of the organizations's positions.[35] Indeed, several studies have found no statistically significant difference between evangelicals and non-evangelicals on attitudes toward most non-religious issues. By late 1982 only 6% of the voters shared the entire agenda of the New Right –

evangelical or otherwise.[36] Since the Evangelical Right thus appeared as divided as other segments of the population over most general political issues, one may conclude that "the term 'evangelical' is rather meaningless when interpreting reactions to general political issues."[37] Moreover, even the most loyal constituency of the Moral Majority has often been apathetic regarding political activity. "Either believing that politics is a dirty business or that such matters should be left in God's hands," they frequently fail to rally when summoned by the organization.[38]

Thus, while the Moral Majority's claims to have "captured" the issues are borne out by most surveys,[39] this phenomenon should be explained by the general turn to the Right in American politics,[40] rather than by the success of the organization and its associates in swaying public attitudes. This is particularly the case with regard to general economic and political issues. In the words of one study, "the available evidence appears to sustain the thesis that the electoral swing toward conservatism and the emergence of a political evangelical movement were parallel developments which may have been mutually reinforcing rather than related to one another as cause and effect."[41] Indeed, the political strength of organizations such as the Moral Majority has been seriously overrated[42] with regard to both general political issues and specific questions affecting Israeli security. Only if a persistent effort by the Religious Right to socialize its constituency to political involvement in general proves successful, will this supportive audience eventually emerge as an important power base for Israel in the American political arena. This did not appear to be the case by the mid-1980s.

C. Summary and Policy Relevancy

The American Jewish community finds itself in a peculiar position. It is in agreement with the Evangelical Right – specifically with the Moral Majority – over the latter's pro-Israel advocacies, yet in disagreement with its domestic agenda.[43] It is in disagreement with liberal churches – e.g., the National Council of Churches – over their pro-PLO and other Middle East positions, yet supports much of their domestic agenda. Arguing against any cooperation with the Moral Majority, a noted Jewish scholar explained that "the continuing interest of the Jew is in exactly the kind of society that makes Mr. Falwell uncomfortable."[44] Sharing that concern, but reaching the opposite conclusion, the chairman of the Conference of Major American Jewish Organizations, Howard M. Squadron, said: "They [Moral Majority] strongly support a lot of things I think are dreadful for the country, but I'm not going to turn away their support of Israel for that."[45]

Several Israeli leaders, specifically of the pre-1984 Likud-led coalition, seemed to share an appreciation of the utility of Moral Majority support and friendship. They have demonstrated unusual deference to the organization's leadership[46] and, on several occasions, have attempted to have it mobilize its communications resources on Israel's behalf.

While the extensive networks of electronic and printed media at its disposal make the Moral Majority a valuable advocate, the organization's impact on the formulation of national policies seems limited. Addressing an audience concerned primarily with the moral and religious dimensions of domestic politics, it has thus far failed to mobilize this audience on behalf of foreign and security measures that concern Israel. Moreover, on the domestic scene its limited success has proved counterproductive from an Israeli point of view: it contributed to the electoral failure of several of Israel's most consistent advocates on Capitol Hill who happened to hold views that ran counter to the organization's preferences on domestic, social and moral issues.

In sum, the Evangelical Right seems to be a permanent phenomenon, and its pro-Israel advocacy is useful. Yet, this utility is limited and its friendship toward Israel may be costly. It may aggravate disagreement within American Jewry and between it and Israel, as well as threaten the political future of Israel's liberal friends in the American political arena.

Chapter 5. The Economy and Foreign/Security Policies

A. Can Foreign Aid Be Spared?

By the early 1980s, the grand total of US foreign aid for the post World War II era exceeded $200 billion. Foreign aid critics argued that the program had actually cost American taxpayers $286 billion in direct spending and "in excess of two trillion dollars when you factor in the interest" paid on federal borrowing for foreign aid.[1] Throughout the decade of the '70s, growing economic concerns at home and failures abroad had strengthened congressional opposition to foreign aid. The American public was consistently and overwhelmingly opposed to it (see Table XX). Americans were questioning the wisdom of spending millions of dollars on failing foreign regimes – with little, if any, return – concurrent with perceived severe shortages in welfare programs inside the US. As one congressman put it: "There is a general feeling the world is ripping us off."[2] The Iranian revolution served to galvanize congressional objections: "Iran was a classic example of our foreign aid being made as an investment. Then a new government overthrew the old, and we wasted all that money."[3] Americans appeared unimpressed with the argument that it was foreign aid that had helped their government "rent" twenty-five years of Iranian cooperation. They seemed equally unimpressed with the fact that the US ranked 17th among the 18 largest industrialized countries (trailed only by Italy) in terms of its relative contribution (by 1982 its total foreign aid program constituted one-fifth of one percent of its total output of goods and services).[4]

Thus, the annual foreign aid measures were featured prominently in the small list of most unpopular items on the congressional calendar. In a clear manifestation of this reality, in 1980 (an election year), due to congressional emphasis on budget-cutting, the FY 1981 foreign aid appropriations bill was never approved. Instead, on December 15, 1980 (only after the elections) Congress cleared a stopgap appropriation which, with some exceptions, provided foreign aid spending at the same level as that proposed on the previous year's bill.[5] Moreover, President Carter's request for foreign aid appropriations for FY 1981 was almost identical to

Table XX

US PUBLIC ATTITUDE TOWARD FOREIGN AID: 1971 - 1980

	Too Much	Too Little
1980	70%	5%
1978	67	4
1977	66	3
1976	76	3
1975	73	5
1974	76	3
1973	70	4
1971	70	4

Source: General Social Survey, National Opinion Research
         Center, University of Chicago, as reported in Opinion
         Outlook, December 8, 1980, p. 3.

his request four years earlier, and constituted a sharp reduction when inflation was taken into account. Reflecting Carter's foreign policy priorities, the figures for military aid are even more instructive: for 1978 Carter requested $973 million (and Congress appropriated $926 million). In 1981 his request was for $895 million.[6]

In sharp contrast with the general trend, throughout the 1970s public and congressional support for aid to Israel was consistent. Even in late 1981, in the thick of the budget-cutting atmosphere (and in the wake of Israel's broadly-condemned bombing of PLO headquarters in Beirut), only 28% of American taxpayers wanted the United States to reduce military aid to Israel; 51% wanted it kept at current levels and 9% wanted it increased.[7] Rather than an aberration, this was a confirmation of a long-held sentiment. In 1978, for example, the majority of Americans polled also felt that aid to Israel was at the right level or too low.[8]

Amplifying on the popularity of aid to Israel in Congress, one observer concluded:

> Each type of foreign aid has its built-in group of supporters and opponents on Capitol Hill....Aid to Israel is popular in both Houses. Without it, the annual foreign aid bills would have little chance of passage.[9]

For this reason, the executive branch has long used aid to Israel as a vehicle for obtaining congressional approval of controversial aid packages. For example, in 1970, "given the popularity of assistance for Israel, the White House felt that the prospects for the passage of the supplementary request were improved because aid for Cambodia, and the $65 million for further aid and assistance for Vietnam were combined with assistance for Israel...."[10] Twelve years later, observers again concluded that the administration's increased aid requests for Israel and Egypt were intended at least partially to serve as "political sweeteners" to help Congress swallow the "bitter foreign aid pill."[11]

Several explanations may be offered for the popularity of aid to Israel with the American public in general, and with Congress in particular. Israel's outstanding record in repaying loans is one. Satisfaction with Jerusalem's success in utilizing the aid – both in terms of economic development and military potency – is another.[12] In addition, specific aid packages have been awarded in order to induce Israel to undertake added security risks and economic losses stemming from the abandonment of territory and other militarily and economically valuable assets in the Sinai. Finally, two most effective lobbies have been involved in energetic efforts to convince congressmen and senators of the utility to American interests of aid to Israel. The one is led by the well-organized, sophisticated and enthusiastic pro-Israel AIPAC (American-Israel Public Affairs Committee); AIPAC has concentrated much of its effort on easing the economic burden of Israel's defense needs. The other is composed – ironically – of the same industrial giants that have long lobbied on behalf of major arms sales to Israel's adversaries (most recently and most aggressively on behalf of the F-15 enhancement and AWACS deal to Saudi Arabia).[13] Since Israel is obliged to spend most FMS (Foreign Military Sales) funds in the US, "the American-Israeli connection is a bonanza for American business....the defense contractors are as eager as the American Jewish Lobby" to have the military portion of the aid bill approved.[14]

These explanations, however, appear to constitute only part of the picture. Rather, it is Israel's unusual popularity with the American public[15] that seems thus far to have led congressmen and senators (as well as recent presidents) to conclude that support for aid to Israel is politically rewarding.

Consequently, Israel's share in US foreign aid – economic and military alike – measured in relative, global terms, has been astonishing (see Tables XXI and XXIII). Considering that Vietnam is no longer a recipient of US aid (and several decades after the termination of the Marshall Plan), Israel, which has long been the leading recipient on a per capita basis – although until 1969 it received aid at an annual rate of under $100 million – is now the leading recipient in overall absolute terms as well (see also Table XXII, as well as Appendix A).

Jerusalem's portion of recently appropriated military aid programs is a case in point. The FY 1981 stopgap appropriations, for example, set a limit of $2,976 million in loans to all foreign recipients put together. Israel was allocated almost half the total amount – $1,400 million (of which $500 million was to be forgiven), compared with the second largest recipient, Egypt – $550 million, and with other regional partners in Washington's strategic design: Oman's $25 million, Somalia's $25 million, and Kenya's $7 million (all three have granted the US access to military facilities on their soil).

Despite the overall reduction in non-military aid, Israel con-

Table XXI

US MILITARY AND ECONOMIC AID: 1946 - 1979[a]
(Current $US)

Over $10 billion:			$1-2 billion:		
Vietnam	$22,877 mil.		Belgium/Luxemburg	$1,737 mil.
Israel[b]	16,628		Bangladesh	1,457
South Korea	12,958		Iran	1,336
			Colombia	1,276
$5-10 billion:			Austria	1,209
France	7,600		Norway	1,170
Turkey	7,138		Portugal	1,119
Egypt	6,380		Chile	1,024
Taiwan	5,977			
Britain	5,682	Under $1 billion:		
India	5,833		Morocco	922
Italy	5,395		Tunisia	875
			Denmark	884
$3-5 billion:			Bolivia	843
Greece	4,894		Pacific Islands	825
Pakistan	4,864		Peru	704
West Germany	3,627		Zaire	697
			Ethiopia	606
$2-3 billion:			Syria	565
Japan	2,890		Dominican Republic	543
Philippines	2,717		Afghanistan	518
Indonesia	2,595		Guatemala	414
Laos	2,509		Poland	404
Brazil	2,465		Sri Lanka	395
Thailand	2,856		Nigeria	392
Jordan	2,159		Panama	380
Yugoslavia	2,155		Ecuador	318
Spain	2,129		New Zealand	3
Netherlands	2,072			
Cambodia	2,051			

Source: Based on US Dept. of State data as presented in US News and World
Report, March 31, 1980, p. 61.

[a]The cost of maintaining US troops in Europe (as well as Japan and South
Korea) may be considered a form of military aid. It is not included in this
table.

Figures do not reflect non-aid military acquisitions. Thus, for example,
Saudi Arabia's military purchases from the US for the years 1976-1982 alone
totalled some $44 billion.

[b]Figures for Israel adjusted based on Appendix A below.

Table XXII

US MILITARY AND ECONOMIC AID TO ISRAEL: FY 1977 - 1983[a]

($million)

Category	1977	1978	1979[b]	1980	1981	1982	1983	Total
Economic Assistance								
Loans	245	260	260	260	--	--	--	1,025
Grants	490	525	525	525	764	806[c]	785	4,420
Total	735	785	785	785	764	806	785	5,445
Military Aid								
Loans	500	500	2700	500	900	850	950	6,900
Grants	500	500	600	500	500	550	750	4,600
Total	1000	1000	3300	1000	1400	1400	1700	11,500
Total Economic & Military Aid								
Loans	745	760	2960	760	900	850	950	7,925
Grants	990	1025	1125	1025	1264	1356	1535	8,320
Grand TOTAL	1735	1785	4085	1785	2164	2206	2485	16,245

Source: Comptroller General of the US, U.S. Assistance to the State of Israel (Washington, DC: GAO, June 24, 1983), pp. 8, 30.

[a]For a more comprehensive list, covering FY 1948-1983, see Appendix A.

[b]1979 increased military aid was related to the Camp David agreement.

[c]This figure includes repayment of $21 million "loaned" by the administration from Israel's $785 million FY 1981 allocation (thus the $764 million figure for that year).

Table XXIII

ISRAEL'S SHARE IN US AID WORLDWIDE:[a] FY 1978-1982

($million)

Fiscal Year	Economic Aid			Military Aid		
	Israel	Worldwide	% to Israel	Israel	Worldwide	% to Israel
1978	785	2,224.4	35.3	1,000.0	2,101.0	47.6
1979	785	1,954.1	40.2	3,300.0[b]	5,673.0	58.2
1980	785	2,158.0	36.4	1,000.0	1,950.0	51.3
1981	764	2,199.2	34.7	1,400.0	3,046.0	46.0
1982	806	2,564.0	31.4	1,400.0	3,833.5	36.5
Total	3,925	11,099.7	35.4	8,100.0	16,603.5	48.8

Sources: Figures for Israel: see Table XXVII above.
Figures for "worldwide:" General Accounting Office, "U.S. Security and Economic Assistance: Programs and Related Activities," (Washington, DC: GAO), June 1, 1982.

[a]The Table does not reflect such aid expenditures as the annual contibution to NATO (officially estimated at $81 billion for FY 1981 alone).

[b]The dramatic increase in military aid was related to the Camp David agreements.

tinued to enjoy generous economic aid as well. Of the total $2.05 billion ESF (Economic Support Fund) approved by the Congress for FY 1981, $785 million were for Israel[16] (and $750 million for Egypt). In appropriating both military and economic aid, Congress again used its authority in Israel's favor: in FY 1981 it added $200 million to President Carter's $1.2 billion request for FMS credits, and made the entire ESF a grant, whereas the administration had requested one-third of it to be in the form of a long-term loan. These were two most generous gestures at a time of increasing domestic economic hardship.

Perhaps even more dramatic were the Reagan administration's request, with the House Foreign Affairs and Senate Foreign Relations committees concurring, for a substantial increase in FY 1983 military aid for Israel. Moreover, the Senate committee also voted a considerable boost in Israel's grant economic aid. Coming in a congressional election year and examined in light of both mounting pressures for reducing the budget deficit, raising taxes and further eliminating popular welfare programs, as well as continued criticism of Israel's foreign/security policy on the West Bank, in southern Lebanon and elsewhere,[17] these measures assume considerable political significance. Indeed, the administration's position on, and congressional deliberations of, the FY 1983 foreign aid bill offer important insights into basic attitudes toward aid for Israel as well as into the economic determinants of Jerusalem's share in the US foreign aid program. Thus, they warrant a detailed examination.[18]

B. FY 1983 Aid Bill: A Revealing Odyssey

As a case study in the problems affecting US aid to Israel in the 1980s, the fate of the 1983 aid bill is as revealing as any we might contemplate. The years 1984 and 1985 witnessed dramatic changes in Israel that clearly affect US aid considerations – the fall of the Likud government, the withdrawal from Lebanon and, most significantly, Israel's economic crisis. But these only serve to accentuate the network of constraints described here with regard both to the US administration and to Israel.

While deliberating the FY 1982 foreign aid budget, and in apparent recognition of the political difficulties of getting a bill enacted in an election year,[19] Congress passed an authorization bill in 1981 that was to cover both FY 1982 and FY 1983. But by early

1982 it was apparent that President Reagan had decided not to yield to the obvious political deterrents; in February 1982 he submitted a new and most ambitious foreign aid budget request for FY 1983. Reflecting the administration's foreign policy orientation and priorities, the request represented a 44% increase over FY 1982 in total (grants and loans) military aid and a much more modest 12% increase in total economic aid. Significantly, the FY 1983 request served to reinforce a trend that originated with Reagan's revision of the Carter administration's request for FY 1982 (see Table XXIV).

The FMS authorization request totalled $5,668 million (a dramatic increase) of which $3,929 million were to be offered in the form of government-guaranteed and subsidized loans.[20] The remaining $1,739 million credits for the purchase of American weapons systems were to be "forgiven," i.e., loans that require no repayment.

Focusing on aid to Israel, the administration asked Congress to increase the total FMS over the previous year by $300 million (justified as a partial compensation for earlier monumental US arms sales to Israel's potential adversaries, most notably to Saudi Arabia), bringing the total to $1,700 million. However, it proposed to cut the "forgiven" (that is, grant) portion of FMS by $50 million, back to its 1981 level of $500 million.

Still, the administration emphasized that "at $1.7 billion, the FY 1983 request [was] 21% above FY 1982 and account[ed] for 44% of U.S. military grants worldwide and 25% of U.S. military credits worldwide."[21]

In the non-military portion of the foreign aid bill, the entire ESF portion totalled $2,886 million, of which $895 million were to be grants. Here too, Israel's share was to be substantial – $785 million. Yet, not only was it identical to the sum appropriated for FY 1982 (thus representing a real decrease when inflation was figured in),[22] but the administration proposed to revert to the pattern prevailing prior to FY 1981 (in both FY 1981 and FY 1982 the entire allocation was not to be repaid), and make one-third of it in the form of loans. The total package of military and economic aid for Israel was thus to reach the unprecedented level of $2,485 million.[23] However, its terms were to be less favorable than in previous years.

In April and May 1982 congressmen appeared once again determined to use their "power of the purse" in Israel's favor.

Table XXIV

FOREIGN AID EMPHASIS: REAGAN vs. CARTER

(Budget Authority in current $million)

	FY 1981 Carter	FY 1982 Carter	FY 1982 Reagan	Reagan Change from FY 1982	Reagan Change from FY 1981
(Grant) Military Assistance Program (MAP)	110.2	33.5	138.5	+313%	+ 25.7%
(Credit) Foreign Military Sales (FMS)	500.0	850.0	1,481.8	+ 74%	+196.4%
Economic Support Fund (ESF)	2,058.45	2,431.5	2,581.5	+ 6%	+ 26.0%
International Military Education and Training (IMET)	28.4	35.7	47.7	+ 34%	+ 68.0%
Peacekeeping Operations (PKO)	25.0	19.0	19.0	--	- 24.0%
TOTAL	2,712.05	3,369.7	4,268.5	+ 27%	+ 57.0%

Sources: Based on "New Directions in Security Assistance," National Security Record, no. 33 (May 1981), p. 3.

First, it was the House Middle East Subcommittee that voted on April 27 to ask the Foreign Affairs Committee to retain both the full $550 million grant portion and the $850 million loan portion allocated to Israel in FY 1982. Moreover, in accepting the administration's proposal for a $300 million increase in total FMS for Israel, the subcommittee recommended that $200 million of it be in the form of a grant. Thus, in voting in favor of the administration's total figure of $1,700 million, the subcommittee brought the grant portion to $750 million – $250 million more than the administration had requested.

A few days later, in its first action on the entire bill, the Foreign Affairs Committee accepted all the recommendations of the Middle East Subcommittee concerning increased military aid to Israel. (Concurrently, the committee curtailed Reagan's request for FMS guarantees for Morocco, by $50 million, and for Tunisia, by $55 million.) Acting on the economic portion of the bill, the committee accepted the president's recommendation for a total ESF for Israel of $785 million but rejected his request that one-third of these funds be repaid. Consequently, if the committee's resolution were to be adopted by the entire Congress, Israel would receive a total aid package equalling the administration's recommendation ($2,485 million), yet the forgiven portion would have been increased to $1,535 million.

Living up to its reputation, and in spite of its chairman's opposition, the Senate Foreign Relations Committee outdid both the administration and the House committee. Arguing that Israel deserved increased American aid to compensate for US arm sales to Arab nations (specifically the AWACS deal to Saudi Arabia), as well as for the loss of energy self-sufficiency and strategic depth stemming from the return of the Sinai to Egypt, the majority on the committee voted to increase the grant portion of FMS to $850 million ($100 million above the House committee's recommendation). In addition, the committee decided to retain the grant form of the proposed ESF and add $125 million to the administration's figure. The Senate committee's version thus recommended a total of $2,610 million, $1,760 million of which were to be granted with no repayment expected (see Table XXV).

Consequently, by late May 1982 it appeared as though neither repeated congressional criticism of Israeli policies in southern Lebanon and on the West Bank nor harsh economic realities at home had affected legislators' determination to increase aid to

Table XXV

US MILITARY AND ECONOMIC AID FOR ISRAEL: FY 1983

($millions)

	Administration's Request	House--Foreign Affairs Committee	Senate--Foreign Relations Committee	Congressional Continuing Resolution
ESF				
Loans	260	0	0	0
Grants	525	785	910	785
Total	785	785	910	785
MSF				
Loans	1200	950	850	950
Grants	500	750	850	750
Total	1700	1700	1700	1700
Total Aid				
Loans	1460	950	850	950
Grants	500	1535	1760	1535
Grand TOTAL	2485	2485	2610	2485

Sources: Congressional Quarterly Almanac, 97th Congress, 2nd Session...1982, Washington, DC. See also, Legislative Update: Year End Report 1982 (Washington, DC: AIPAC, December 23, 1982), p. 13.

105

Israel. Yet, less than one month later, while most observers focused their attention on events in the region – predicting that alleged excessive Israeli use of force would prompt Congress to utilize foreign aid to punish Jerusalem – it was primarily in the American economic context that the change occurred.

On June 23, 1982 Congress enacted its first Budget Resolution establishing budget-targets for FY 1983 (beginning October 1, 1982). The resolution called for deficit reduction measures amounting to $76.8 billion in FY 1983. It set limits of $15.9 billion in budget authority and $11.5 billion in outlays for international affairs programs. With foreign aid the biggest item in that category, this meant an actual freeze at FY 1982 level or below, as the limits for that year were $16.75 billion in budget authority and $11.4 billion in outlays. Equally significant was the fact that this resolution imposed far greater limitations on outlays – that is funds to be spent in the given fiscal year – than on total obligational authority (TOA), which authorizes spending that may take several years to disburse. In light of the fact that aid to Israel and Egypt consists mostly of outlays, Democrats and some Republican legislators – with explicit support from President Reagan – tried to boost the foreign aid figures by $600 million to protect aid for these two countries. When it appeared that this issue threatened to block passage of the entire budget resolution, the president yielded and supporters of the increased figure lost by the narrowest margin possible. Thus the resolution left Congress with three major options:

1. Reduce multilateral development aid programs. Since these programs spend their funding slowly, a drastic cut would have been necessary to yield the desired increased funding for programs that are characterized by swift outlays.

2. Reject all proposals for increases in aid to Israel (and Egypt) and, if need be, cut this program even further.

3. Fail to pass a new aid authorization bill for FY 1983.

The first option was most appealing to congressional conservatives. Having consistently objected to American contributions to multilateral development aid projects, they could not but welcome cuts in them. Liberals, however, without whom the entire bill could not pass, were faced with a difficult choice: they have long been committed to these programs, and have fought hard on behalf of them; they consider them essential for US foreign policy.

As to the second option, it was recommended by the few

foreign-aid supporters who argued against the overwhelming concentration of Economic Support Funds in three Middle East countries (Israel, Egypt, Turkey), and in favor of disbursing these funds among the less developed countries which buy 39% of all US exports.[24] Yet, as suggested above, a decision to cut aid to Israel (and Egypt) was considered not only likely to jeopardize passage of the entire bill, but would also obviate the need for the new authorization legislation altogether. Since, as noted above, in 1981 Congress had already passed FY 1983 authorization legislation, no new act was required for aid to continue at FY 1982 levels. (Ironically, from Israel's point of view, the prospect of no new legislation appeared at least as attractive as unqualified enactment of the administration's request for FY 1983. For while the President had offered to raise Israel's overall package by a very significant $300 million, he had also proposed a substantial reduction of the grant portion).

For all these reasons, the third option appeared the least objectionable to most Washington legislators.[25] Moreover, by September 1982, Israel's conduct in Lebanon and its rejection of President Reagan's proposal for the next phase in the Arab-Israel peace process left Congress with little enthusiasm for a fight on behalf of aid to Israel.

Yet in making a distinction between Israel, the people, and Israel, the government, the American legislature once again appeared to be guided by the basic characteristics of its attitude toward the Jewish state: support for its well-being even when criticizing its policies. Congressional conferees used unprecedentedly blunt language in criticizing Israeli policies – specifically actions affecting the demographic balance on the West Bank – while nevertheless adopting the administration's suggested overall increased figure and imposing upon it the House's version of improved terms (see Table XXV above). Moreover, in rejecting the more dramatic improvements suggested by the Senate, legislators welcomed erroneous interpretations of their chosen course of action. They were quite pleased with suggestions that what had been rejected primarily for economic reasons was actually an expression of congressional displeasure with Israel.

C. Conclusions and Policy Relevancy

By the end of President Reagan's second year in office, Americans, though still supportive of the administration's extravagant projections for defense build-up, began to exhibit an awareness of the costly trade-off between defense appropriations on the one hand, and welfare programs and government services on the other.[26] Moreover, the assumption that greater expenditure automatically yielded greater security was also being challenged.[27] At that time these trends were still confined to a small minority, but they had to be considered early signs of potential vulnerabilities ahead.

In the meantime, defense spending seemed the lone survivor of the budget-cutting mood projected from the White House and infecting Congress. Consequently, those areas of the US defense build-up that – either directly or indirectly – affected Israeli security, continued to enjoy generous allocations. However, even if maintained, the implications of this trend for Israeli security were not unidirectional. In the short term Israel stood to benefit from both the image and, eventually, the possible reality of a more potent America that proved determined to invest in as well as produce and utilize the instruments of power relevant to Southwest Asian contingencies. The potential consequences of such a trend would include the following:

- An improved American capability to reach remote "hot spots" in time and with adequate firepower to affect developments;
- an adequate capacity for the US to resupply allies under crisis conditions (independent of en-route facilities);
- greater willingness on the part of a more confident US to meet threats – or actual challenges – to western interests in Southwest Asia;
- continued American ability to provide friends with newer generations of military technology and hardware; and
- an increased readiness among states in the region – their confidence in the credibility of American commitments boosted – to collaborate with Washington's strategic regional designs.[28]

Moreover, in the near future, while the instruments of power – particularly those relevant to rapid conventional force projection – are in production, the newly assertive America will continue actively to seek regional assistance to augment its own shortfalls in air- and sea-lift capabilities. Under these circumstances, the role of politically stable, militarily potent, technologically advanced and reliably pro-western regional allies as strategic assets may be enhanced. Even if taken for granted and all-too-often troublesome, Israel's potential contribution in this context escapes but a few in Washington.

Yet, even during this transitory stage, Washington can hardly be expected to shun other offers of strategic cooperation. These will inevitably yield greater military intimacy with some of Israel's regional foes. Moreover, with the gradual evolution of the necessary means of self-sufficiency in rapid force projection, at the very time that the benefits of the above-listed advantages can be fully enjoyed by Israel, Washington's acute need for such allies is likely to decline. In an era where Israel's historical and moral legacies are less relevant to shaping American attitudes and policies than its present moral image and perceived contribution to American interests,[29] such a development should be carefully monitored as an important predictor of future relations. Further, if erosion in US public support for defense spending continues over the long term, Israel will be one of many US partners affected.

This reality is even more immediately relevant to American aid. The odyssey of the FY 1983 foreign aid legislation serves as a most illuminating illustration of the process by which determinants of an exclusively domestic character – the political (and economic) costs of budget deficits – affect the magnitude of foreign aid.[30] Those interested in the fate of future legislated aid for Israel should note the FY 1983 precedent, whereby increases were curtailed due to such considerations. These are particularly relevant to assessments of the net contribution of American aid with the termination of the ten-year grace period on repayment of the post Yom Kippur War loans. By the mid-1980s annual payments of principal and interest exceeded $1 billion.[31] Yet another significant precedent was established when Congress was willing to encourage an erroneous interpretation of its final decision.[32] On the one hand, repeated expressions of congressional hostility toward certain Israeli foreign/security policymakers have not produced a noticeable reduction in the extent of support for aid to Israel on Capitol Hill. On the other hand, however, the changing, younger Congress,[33] in linking blunt criticism of Israeli policies to the provision of generous aid, suggested that a spillover effect was quite possible: in the face of objectionable Israeli conduct, foreign aid might not be spared.

Chapter 6. Oil and Petrodollars: The Role of Perceptions and Big Business

A. Energy and Foreign/Security Policies

At the conclusion of a major research project sponsored jointly by Harvard University's Center for Science and International Affairs and the Energy and Environmental Policy Center, the two experts who coordinated the study presented their findings, beginning with the facts: "When the seventies began, Americans imported 3.5 million barrels of oil a day....But by the end of that distressing decade, we were importing 8.5 million barrels per day....Our dependence on oil imports increased 250% between 1973 and 1979.[1] Others in American academia and the business community concurred and forecasted that in the absence of a drastic change, "...the United States would be even more dependent on imported oil in the 1980s"[2] (see Table XXVI and Figure 2).

Such pessimistic predictions were common in the American media of the late 1970s. They drew both on figures provided by the business community and on equally speculative official studies. In December 1979 the Permanent Select Committee on Intelligence of the US House of Representatives released a committee report entitled "Intelligence on the World Energy Future," which contained the following statement:

> The consensus of witnesses before the sub-committee foresees a world shortage of oil in the near term. Fundamentally, during the next three to six years demand for oil is expected to grow while the supply of oil will increase only slightly, if at all, whatever the price offered....The date on which this shortage will set in remains a point of conjecture. The Central Intelligence Agency expects it before 1982 and forecasts an average excess of demand over supply of two to five million barrels per day.[3]

The testimony reflected the findings of a study conducted by the Central Intelligence Agency. It placed projected demand for Saudi Arabia's oil for 1982 at between 11.7 and 16.2 million barrels per day (MBD).[4] This broad margin of uncertainty (4.5 MBD) was expanded further by the Congressional Budget Office (CBO) which, using CIA's own data, demonstrated that the demand for Saudi oil

Table XXVI

EXXON'S PROJECTIONS FOR 1980

Date of Projection	Free World Oil Consumption	US Oil Consumption
April 1977	76 MBD	23.6 MBD
April 1978	72 MBD	20.4 MBD
December 1979	60 MBD	16.4 MBD
December 1980	55 MBD[a]	16.0 MBD[b]

Source: William M. Brown, <u>Can OPEC Survive the Glut?</u> Hudson Institute Research Memorandum No. 112 (New York, October 1981), p. 6.

[a]The actual demand for 1980 was 50 MBD. The April 1977 projection was thus exaggerated by 52% vis-à-vis actual December 1980 consumption.

[b]Actual consumption confirms this final projection. The April 1977 projection was thus exaggerated by 44% vis-à-vis actual December 1980 consumption.

111

Figure 2

PROJECTIONS OF UNITED STATES ENERGY CONSUMPTION TO 1990

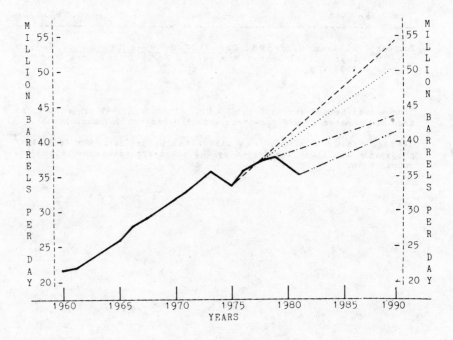

Historical Consumption
1975-76 Projections   — — — — —
1977-78 Projections   ·················
1979-80 Projections   —·—·—·—·—·
1981-82 Projections   —··—··—··—·

YEARS

Source: Two Energy Futures: A National Choice of the 80s,
          (Washington, DC: The American Petroleum Institute),
          1982, p. 19.

could be as high as 22.2 MBD.[5] Consequently, forecasts of in-creased American imports were coupled with projections of ever-increasing demand for oil – particularly OPEC's and specifi-cally Saudi Arabia's. Americans were thus faced with the political consequences of yet another decade of dependence, i.e., a shrink-ing capability to pursue independent policies on issues dear to OPEC members.

One manifestation of the effect of such perceptions on decisions made in Washington involved the Strategic Petroleum Reserve (SPR). Designed to alleviate the short-term impact of an interrup-tion in the flow of oil to the US, thus at least partially deterring a politically-motivated embargo, the SPR triggered angry Saudi objections. According to some reports Saudi officials viewed the SPR as "a threat to their country," fearing that "with a billion barrels of oil in the reserve the United States would be more reluctant to go to the aid of Saudi Arabia if [it] were threatened." In addition, Saudi officials were reportedly convinced that "the less oil that the United States has in its reserve, the greater power the Saudis might exercise over American foreign policy."[6] During the Carter years, Washington's initial response was a decision first to stop, and, later, not to resume, purchases for the SPR.[7] By 1980 the administration had initiated a proposal that was judged by some administration officials to "give the Saudis an unprecedented degree of control over the use of the U.S. oil stockpile,"[8] in return for a Saudi decision not to cut back on production. But Riyadh was not satisfied. In the words of a *Washington Post* report, it "sent" US Energy Secretary Charles Duncan "packing,"[9] triggering a wave of angry editorials in the American press.[10] They all expressed the sentiment that "neither friendship nor market stability can mean much if they act as bars on U.S. security."[11]

However, by mid-1981 and, even more so, during 1982, with the actual figures for 1981 available, it became apparent that neither academia, nor the oil industry, nor the US government was immune to error. OPEC's output for 1981 declined 16.6%, following a 12.9% decline in 1980[12] (see Figure 3); Saudi Arabia's own production was 20% less than a year before;[13] world consumption fell dramatically to a level lower than in 1973;[14] and the 21 industrial states that are members of the International Energy Agency (IEA) reduced their dependence on imported oil by almost 20% in two years.[15] As for the US (see Table XXVII), its oil consumption declined 6.2% in one year,[16] and 11% over the period

113

Figure 3

CRUDE OIL PRODUCTION:

OPEC VERSUS FREE WORLD NON-OPEC, 1973-1982

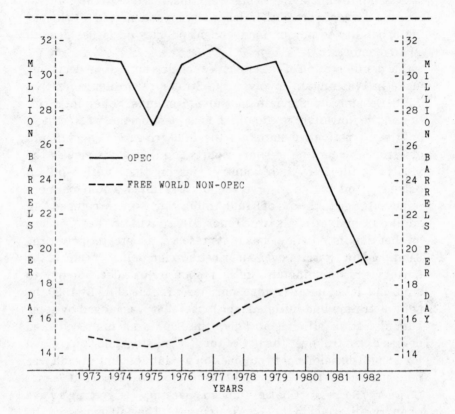

1982 DATA ARE FIRST SIX MONTHS

Source: Based on Energy Security for the United States: Progress, Pitfalls, Potential (Washington, DC: American Petroleum Institute), September 1982, p. 39.

114

Table XXVII

US OIL IMPORTS: 1981; 1982

	1981[a]		1982[b]	
	1st Quarter	2nd Quarter	1st Quarter	2nd Quarter
TOTAL (MBD)	5,249.2	4,975.4	4,039.0	3,402.2
Source (% share of total)				
Middle East[c]	28.1	24.3	26.2	20.0
Africa	33.4	35.4	24.7	14.2
Other OPEC	10.9	10.2	9.8	12.2
TOTAL OPEC	72.4%	69.9%	60.7%	46.4%[d]
Mexico	8.2	10.4	13.5	20.9
North Sea	7.4	9.5	8.8	14.5
Other non-OPEC	12.0	10.2	17.0	18.2
TOTAL NON-OPEC	27.6%	30.1%	39.3%	53.6%

Sources: Based on Dapei Meida (Israel Institute of Petroleum and Energy) No. 53 (October 3, 1982), pp. 4, 5. See also "Mexico Displaces Saudi Arabia," Petroleum Economist, September 1982, pp. 352-353.

[a] During the first half of 1981 imported oil constituted 35% of US oil consumption; 15% of total US energy consumption.

[b] During the first half of 1982 imported oil constituted 25% of US oil consumption; 11% of total US energy consumption.

[c] Saudi Arabia's share in US imports declined 50% during this period.

[d] This was the first time in ten years that OPEC's share in US imports was less than 50%.

1980-1982.[17] Concurrently, its oil imports declined by 30.5% over the period 1979-1981,[18] reaching just under 5.5 MBD (compared with the 1977 peak of 8.6 MBD).[19] Imports continued to decline throughout 1982 and 1983,[20] representing a 34% decline for the period 1980-1982. By late 1983 US imports averaged less than 4.2 MBD; imports from OPEC nations dropped to 28% of their 1977 levels.[21]

The decline in US oil imports (see Figure 4) started in 1977 when foreign oil sources supplied 45% of total US oil consumption and 22% of total energy consumption. By the first half of 1982 these imports had been reduced to 25% of total oil consumption and 11% of total energy consumption.[22] Similar trends can be observed concerning American imports from the Middle East (OAPEC and Iran). They peaked in 1977 at 3.7 MBD, constituting 20.2% of US oil consumption; by the first quarter of 1982 these imports fell to 1.1 MBD, thus constituting less than 7% of US oil consumption, less than 3% of total US energy usage,[23] and 20% of total US oil imports (see Table XXVIII).

Significantly, even this lower rate of import enabled the US to more than double the SPR.[24] Consequently, as of mid-1981 an increasing number of studies concluded that fundamental structural changes had taken place in the oil and energy markets. The combined impact of (1) alternatives for oil, (2) energy efficiency and conservation, and (3) increased non-OPEC production, was judged to have produced a world-wide oil glut that was expected to outlast the modest rate of growth in most consumer nations.[25] Prospects for expanded post-war Iranian and Iraqi production reinforced these predictions.

"The current oil glut is hardly a temporary aberration," concluded a late-1981 Hudson Institute study; it suggested that "not only are world oil prices likely to decline during the next few years, but even a collapse of prices cannot be ruled out."[26] While this study was in a minority in predicting a collapse of prices, its prediction of a decline was shared by many.[27] Such predictions yielded the very optimistic conclusion that "the oil importing countries are likely to become less vulnerable to supply interruptions."[28] Put more bluntly, by mid-1981 a major publication oriented toward the American business community asked:

> What if the Arabs turn off the spigot again?...gasoline rationing, other conservation moves, and a drawdown of the free world's near record oil inventories could keep the

Figure 4

US OIL IMPORTS: 1972-1982

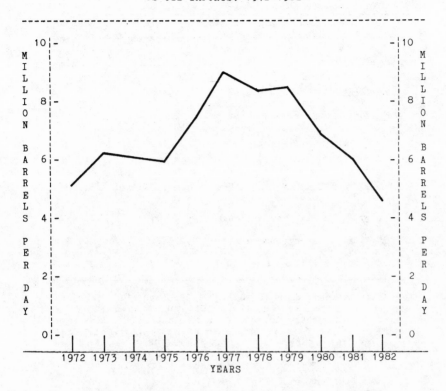

YEARS

1982 DATA ARE FIRST SIX MONTHS

Sources: US Department of Energy, Monthly Energy Review (Wash-
           ington, DC, May 1982) as quoted in Energy Security for
           the United States: Progress, Pitfalls, Potential (Wash-
           ington, DC: American Petroleum Institute), September
           1982, p. 15.

Table XXVIII

US OIL IMPORTS: 1977 vs. 1982

	1977	1982[a]
Total Imports	8.6 MBD	5.5 MBD
% of Total US Oil Consumption	45%	25%
% of Total US Energy Consumption	22%	11%
Middle East Imports (OAPEC & Iran)	3.7 MBD	1.1 MBD
% of Total US Oil Consumption	20.2%	6.9%
% of Total US Energy Consumption	9.7%	2.9%
% of Total US Oil Imports	43.0%	20.0%

Sources: National Journal, July 20, 1982, p. 1106; February 20, 1982, p. 325. Eliahu Kanovsky, "The Diminishing Impact of Middle East Oil: A Harbinger of the Future?" in Colin Legum, ed., Middle East Contemporary Survey, 5 (1980-1981) (New York and London: Holmes & Meier), 1982, p. 376; Dapei Meida, No. 53 (October 3, 1982), p. 4.

[a] Actual figures for 1st quarter.

industrialized world running for many months to come....

In the new oil-supply situation that has developed, Washington will inevitably have more leverage on the Saudis to make demands that would enhance mutual security.[29]

An equally extreme version of the optimistic school was a popular cover story in a late 1981 American monthly which reached the conclusion encapsulated in its title: "In Case You Missed It... The Energy Crisis is Over."[30] The article blamed earlier US price controls for having perpetuated the "artificially low price of domestic oil," thus discouraging expensive new explorations. It attributed the decline in US imports, the resulting contribution to the glut in the world oil market, and prospects for a real decline in the cost of energy, to the "new realism" that governed President Reagan's January 28, 1981 decision to bring an immediate end to these price controls. The study concluded that a similar move to deregulate the price of natural gas would yield further production and a decrease of some 2 MBD in US oil imports. "Without the foreign oil needed to make up for the natural gas shortage," the article predicted, "OPEC would be about as important to the American economy as a Turkish bazaar."[31]

This article was important for two reasons. First, it was representative of a new, albeit hesitant, wave of popular thinking on the issue. While at the time of its publication the American media had yet to embrace such conclusions, this new wave[32] signaled a change in perceptions of the degree of US dependence on decisions made by members of OPEC – hence, a prospect of greater confidence in America's freedom of action and ability to alter relevant policies.[33] Second, the article reflected the thinking of the Reagan administration. In the words of Danny J. Boggs, Executive Secretary of the Cabinet Council on Natural Resources and Environment, the way the Energy Department's regulatory machinery of the 1970s worked was: "Every time people bought Saudi Arabian oil, other Americans wrote them a check." If there had been a market-oriented energy policy to begin with, he said, "I don't think you would hear that we have an energy problem today."[34] On the question of natural gas as well, the administration's position supported the article's argument: "There is much more gas than previously believed. Because natural gas prices are being held below free-market levels there is less incentive to explore for new gas reserves."[35]

The Reagan administration's obvious free market approach to

energy policy[36] assumed that at reasonable prices (as determined by supply and demand) US domestic production of oil and natural gas would decrease, consumption (due to price-imposed conservation) would decrease, and energy independence could be achieved. A dramatic surge in exploration,[37] as well as the continued decline in consumption, were presented as supportive evidence.

Although assessments of US energy potential are essential for any prediction of American dependence on outside sources, they are beyond the scope of the present study. Suffice it to quote critics of the administration's policy who raised the question: "What will happen when the new administration's supply-side theories bump into the hard geological reality of the energy predicament – which is, simply put, that this country is running out of oil?...to raise expectations that decontrol will solve this problem by bringing on a torrent of new oil is to base public policy on Disney's First Law: 'Wishing Will Make It So'!"[38]

The degree of uncertainty and record of errors that have long typified projections of energy markets focus attention on the variable that is most relevant to the formulation of related public attitudes as well as foreign and security policies: it is the *perception* of dependence that affects decisions, rather than any objective factual dependence. Most consistent in contributing to the perception of continued and growing dependence into the next century has been the American oil industry.[39] Within the US government, as late as 1981 both Department of Energy and Pentagon officials were found also to hold such views. At the same time, energy experts and some Middle East experts in both the Department of State and the National Security Council, were identified with the optimistic school.[40] Three years later, on Capitol Hill, the memory of long lines at the gasoline pumps was reportedly still affecting legislators' inclinations concerning future energy shortages.[41]

Moreover, even the assumption of a potential total energy independence for the US has not been accepted by some as satisfying the minimum requisites for energy independence. For example, although it recognized the continuing increase in non-OPEC supplies in the face of declining world-wide demand, a late 1980 Senate staff report argued that the US approach to energy problems had been focused on the wrong problem. Finding sources to provide for US needs, it argued, would not solve the national security problems that affect the economies of America's western allies. "Energy independence – the notion that if the United States can just eliminate the oil imports, everything will be all right – is an illusion, at least for the foreseeable future."[42] The underlying assumption of the report was that as oil-consuming nations reduce their import needs through conservation and alternate energy development, the producing countries can reduce production levels, thus maintaining their leverage over the West. While recent analyses[43] and mounting evidence make convincing arguments to the contrary, perceptions of dependence are still widespread.[44]

Yet, it is not only those who accept the more pessimistic assumptions and fall into the alarmist category who emphasize the threat to US national security and foreign policy stemming from dependence on energy sources located in the remote and demonstrably unstable Persian Gulf. Even among the optimists, perceptions of promising trends do not translate into instantaneous relief. Recognition of the potential for adverse developments taking place before these processes reach fruition – in terms of the US' own as well as America's allies' independence – produces considerable concern. It differs from that of the extremists in the projected scope and duration of continued dependence. More important, it differs in discounting a voluntary interruption – that is, a politically-motivated embargo. Yet, it does not dispute the assessed consequences of an involuntary interruption occurring prior to the attainment of substantial western energy independence.

This concern found its expression in the US Energy Department's bi-annual review submitted to the US Congress in February 1982. It forecast that "during the 1980s, considerable reliance on Middle Eastern oil [was] expected to continue. Therefore, any substantial disruption in oil supply could have a major adverse impact on importing nations, including the United States."[45]

By the mid-1980s, optimists and pessimists seemed to be in greater agreement than ever before. Their consensus also applied to the important question of possible voluntary interruption. In a major departure from the common wisdom of the 1970s, Americans of the alarmist school have increasingly accepted the conclusion of the optimists that changing circumstances have already affected the freedom of action of oil producers.[46] Consequently, while sudden supply interruptions and drastic price increases were not ruled out, it was assumed they would not originate with a conscious Saudi decision triggered by policy differences with the US. Rather, a regional conflict, revolution, accident, sabotage or natural disaster were mentioned as possible causes.[47]

When translated into concrete policies, even among most alarmists and certainly among optimists, the traditional linkage between Saudi oil policies, US energy needs, and America's position on the Arab-Israeli dispute was no longer as firm and automatic as it had been during the 1970s. By the mid-1980s, many Americans still suggested that a resolution of the Palestinian issue could remove one cause for Middle East instability, and an irritant from US-OAPEC (Arab members of OPEC) relations. However, this was suggested within the context of overall US regional and global strategies rather than as a direct derivative of energy requirements. The idea that progress within the Arab-Israel peace process was a prerequisite for assured western access to oil at reasonable prices, or that the absence of progress on the Palestinian question was a major threat to oil supplies – a notion widely held by the Carter administration – was no longer entertained. The Iran-Iraq war, the Soviet invasion of Afghanistan, as well as the Ka'ba affair and other incidents that demonstrated Saudi vulnerabilities, were all offered as examples for more likely, non-Arab-Israel-related threats to stability and the flow of oil.[48]

Concurrently, Saudi *economic* considerations were better understood as determinants of Riyadh's price and production policies. This conclusion received unusually candid support from no less than the Saudi daily *Al-Riyadh*. On June 13, 1982, shortly after the Israeli invasion of Lebanon, the paper responded to Arab urgings for Saudi economic sanctions against the US, saying that while such sanctions would have no impact on the American economy, they might be dangerous to Riyadh.[49] Repeated references in the American press to a speech by Saudi Arabia's Oil Minister Sheikh Ahmed Zaki Yamani to students and faculty of the Dahran University of Petroleum and Minerals, testified to this evolving trend as well. Yamani explained that

> ...price rises...were accelerating the search in the West for alternative energy sources. If this continued, it would only take seven to ten years before the demand even for low-cost Saudi oil would not be enough to finance Saudi development needs.
>
> The interest of the kingdom is that we extend the life of oil to

the longest extent possible to allow us to build our economy in the most diversified manner... If we don't do that, we will reach a time when there will be a violent shakeup in our country.[50]

Still, long-held public perceptions were slow in changing. Despite evidence to the contrary, toward the mid-1980s concern for a possible voluntary cutoff in the flow of oil imposed by Persian Gulf states continued to color perceptions of Middle East events. Fear of a cutoff caused by external aggression yielded support for military countermeasures. Fear of a cutoff imposed for political reasons still affected public attitudes toward the Arab-Israel conflict. By late 1983, even the renewed emphasis on the SPR, then holding over 380 million barrels (equalling seven months of imports from OPEC sources or 900 days of imports from the Persian Gulf at then current rates of import),[51] was not sufficiently reassuring for a concerned consumer. This ambivalence between growing intellectual confidence stemming from increasing exposure to optimistic studies, on the one hand, and emotional concern resulting from vivid memories of a decade of pessimistic assessments and experiences on the other, seemed likely to characterize American public attitudes on relevant issues for the remainder of the 1980s.

B. Petrodollars and Foreign/Security Policies

The "decade of OPEC," beginning with the quadrupling of oil prices that accompanied the 1973-1974 oil embargo, produced a related phenomenon that is as relevant to the formulation of US Middle East policies as the question of energy supply itself. It is the growing influence and political relevancy of OAPEC petrodollars and of those who benefit most from them.

By late 1981 the issue rose in the American public consciousness to the extent that the largest number of respondents (70%) to a Gallup poll identified oil companies as the pressure group that exerted too much political influence in the US.[52] Concurrently, accurate information and detailed data about OAPEC investments in the US were hard to come by. Time and again the American media voiced the frustration of those interested in the subject, suggesting that it was not the American public alone, but, allegedly, the US government, too, that did not have "any idea of how much of America [was] owned by OPEC countries."[53] The absence of sufficient data did not prevent – perhaps even encouraged – popular perceptions that the very magnitude of its holdings and the presumed consequences of withdrawing them, gave OAPEC "effective working control of the American Banking system."[54]

Indeed, in the early 1980s reliable figures on Saudi or other individual Persian Gulf states' purchases and investments in the US were impossible to obtain. Accurate, detailed data became less available as early as 1973, with the first wave of increased Arab investments in the US. Arguing that the wealth of data precluded specificity, the administration lumped together "Middle East Oil Exporters" in official reports. This initial explanation was later to give way to another – that disaggregation was precluded by pledges of confidentiality to individual investors – and the practice continued. Media, and more significantly, congressional protestations have had little impact. Failing to produce a change in administration attitude on this issue, Rep. Benjamin Rosenthal (D: New York) introduced legislation in summer 1982 to lift the veil of secrecy surrounding such investments. By the mid-1980s his – and others' – efforts were yet to produce any meaningful results.

A February 1975 memo from the under-secretary of the treasury explained the administration's reasoning. It stated that "the *sine qua non* for the Saudi [was] confidentiality and we have assured them that we will do everything in our power to comply with their desires."[55] These assurances had been given in early 1974 in negotiations conducted by Secretary of the Treasury William E. Simon. According to Mr. Simon, "this regional reporting was the only way in which Saudi Arabia would agree" to the purchase of US securities.[56]

Aggregating data for groups of OAPEC members has been the most serious difficulty, but not the only one. Significant gaps and incompatibilities exist even within the less useful, aggregated data.[57] Thus, for example, deposits in foreign branches of American banks or investments made via intermediaries are not included.[58] Consequently, most assessments of purchases and holdings of specific OAPEC states border on speculation. As to the group as a whole, according to the US Department of the Treasury, Arab investments in the United States at the end of June 1981 approached $60 billion.[59] Adding OAPEC members' recorded end-of-March 1981 deposits in foreign branches of American banks – $18.4 billion – and the unrecorded transactions, the figure probably exceeded $100 billion.[60] Most estimates suggest that the Saudis alone account for well over one-half of all Arab investments.[61]

Considered in relative terms the holdings of OAPEC members may appear less significant than is commonly assumed. Their respective investments account for less than one-quarter of all foreign holdings of US government securities; less than 4% of the total debt of the US Treasury; less than 2% of total US bank deposits; less than 1% of the total investments in corporate stocks and bonds and less than 1% of total direct foreign investments.[62] Yet, these seemingly modest proportions are quite misleading. On the one hand, a strong case can be made for the ability of the American financial system and the US dollar to survive a sudden, massive sale of securities or withdrawal of deposits from American banks. Moreover, not only are the American system and dollar capable of absorbing such a blow, but for very good reasons of self-interest and dependence on these two American institutions, it may be assumed that OAPEC members are unlikely to inflict such a blow.[63] On the other hand, neither the magnitude of possible disruption nor the potential for other than economically motivated acts on the part of OAPEC can be overestimated. Certainly, the role of perceptions should not be ignored. In the words of a Senate Foreign Relations Committee staff report: "Saudi Arabia did not hesitate to use the oil weapon against the United States in the last Mid-East war, despite earlier warm U.S.-Saudi relations; there is no guarantee that next time they won't wield the money weapon, too."[64]

In sum, it appears that both expert analyses and, more significantly, common perceptions attribute considerable political potency to possible threats of sudden withdrawals of Arab petrodollars invested in the American economy.

Similarly obscure – and equally important politically – have been American investments in the Middle East. Department of Commerce figures on direct investments list only two Arab countries separately – Egypt and Libya. The more significant targets for American investment – Saudi Arabia, Kuwait and the United Arab Emirates – are again grouped together with Iran, Bahrain, Iraq, Oman and Qatar under the heading "Middle East OPEC."[65] The only useful figures are on US bank claims in the region, as provided by the Federal Reserve Bank. Here, too, in relative terms the figures may appear insignificant: less than 3% of total foreign lending by American banks.[66] Yet considering the fact that financial interactions are overwhelmingly concentrated with the six largest American banks,[67] both the incentive and capacity of these six institutions for responsiveness to their customers become evident.[68]

Politically-motivated sudden withdrawals of substantial deposits or massive sales of securities is only one area of petrodollar-related concerns. Another is the matter of foreign control over sensitive industries. Although most direct Arab investments in the US have been in real estate, some have established Arab control over banks,[69] while others have enabled Arabs to gain control over oil refineries or over companies specializing in the exploration and development of natural resources.[70] The most significant – both financially and politically – was the December 1981 Kuwait Petroleum Corporation (KPC) takeover of Sante Fe International Corporation. Representing the largest single investment in US industry by an OPEC government, the $2.5 billion transaction placed a leading oil and gas-drilling contractor under the control of an Arab government. Yet it was the involvement of the company's subsidiary, C.F. Braun, in designing three plutonium-producing facilities owned by the US Department of Energy that drew public attention to the deal. Indeed, this may explain the Kuwaiti interest in Santa Fe International itself, as a previous Kuwaiti attempt to purchase C.F. Braun directly fell through. This transaction could provide Kuwait with access to classified information in a most sensitive area.[71]

Finally, a third field of concern – and largely a by-product of the other two – has been the indirect leverage applied by OAPEC members, using the "good offices" of the many hundreds of US corporations that enjoy the economic benefits of US-OAPEC relations.

Even prior to the dramatic increase of 1973 in the presumed reward for pro-OAPEC policies, American business executives were engaged in efforts to lure US Middle East policies to a course more favorable to their Arab clients. Thus, for example, shortly after the June 1967 war, L.F. McCollum, Chairman of the Board of Continental Oil Company, tried to impress upon Walter Rostow, President Johnson's national security advisor, his company's long-advocated need "to demonstrate that the United States was not wholly one-sided in the Arab-Israeli dispute."[72]

Similarly, two years later, a group of senior oil and other major business company executives lobbied President Nixon and his NSC adviser, Henry A. Kissinger, for a more "even-handed" Middle East policy. During the final phase of preparations for the unveiling of the Rogers Plan they argued for an immediate American initiative designed to improve US relations with the oil-producing Arab countries.[73] And during the 1973 October War, US oil companies provided Saudi Arabia with information about the sources of oil supplies to the US military, thus allegedly enabling the embargo to be expanded beyond its original scope.[74] Yet, the major wave of oil (and other business) executives' involvement in attempts to shape American perceptions of, and policies toward, the Middle East began in the mid-1970s.

Initial approaches by oil companies to their stockholders asking them to lobby for an "even-handed" American Middle East policy were documented in 1974-75, along with pro-Saudi appeals to the American public in the form of paid advertisements in major publications.[75] These were followed by substantial contributions to leading American universities as well as to Arab and pro-Arab organizations in the US and in the Middle East. The latter efforts were directed primarily toward facilitating activities geared to educating the American public concerning Arab preferences within the Arab-Israel context.[76] Documents subpoenaed from ARAM-CO (the oil consortium consisting of Mobil, Exxon, Texaco, and Standard Oil of California) by the Senate Subcommittee on Multinational Corporations revealed that it was in response to specific Saudi demands that many of these activities had been undertaken.[77] By 1978 American corporations were already involved in intensive lobbying on behalf of Saudi Arabia's arms purchases in the US.[78] Yet, the direct link between petrodollars and the involvement of the American business community with specific decisions in US foreign and security policies, was exemplified significantly during the 1981 debate over the administration's intention to sell Saudi Arabia auxiliary systems geared to enhancing the offensive utility of Riyadh's 52 F-15 Eagle aircraft. Better known as the AWACS deal, the proposed transaction emerged as the first major legislative test for the Reagan administration's foreign policy. More significantly, however, it turned out to be a turning point in the determination and ability of the business community to mobilize support on behalf of an economically-motivated stand on a national security question.

Publicly, it was Mobil Oil Corporation, long known for its

intimacy with the ruling Saudi family,[79] that led the campaign. During the final phase of the campaign alone, Mobil spent over half a million dollars on a series of full-page advertisements in at least twenty-six US newspapers and magazines.[80] Focusing on "the profound and rapidly growing economic partnership between the United States and Saudi Arabia," Mobil's advertisement campaign included the suggestion that "the widespread debate...about future American foreign policy concerning Saudi Arabia" threatened "a flourishing network of Saudi investments and Saudi trade involving hundreds of American businesses" and covered "virtually the entire spectrum of US commerce," including contracts for work in Saudi Arabia "well in excess of $35 billion." According to these statements, hundreds of thousands of jobs for American workers in forty-two states were at stake.

This last theme – jobs for Americans – was the main vehicle for an ambitious and effective nationwide campaign of business interests. A group of three registered agents for Saudi Arabia[81] and two Saudi officials[82] directed the campaign. With the help of Senate Majority Leader Howard Baker, it identified the specific contractors or subcontractors residing in each state and prepared lists for American firms to contact their state senators. Led primarily by major AWACS contractors – United Technologies and the Boeing Company of Seattle – hundreds of chief executive officers and corporate presidents approached their senators in an effort to impress upon them the specific loss to be incurred by their own constituencies if the $8.5 billion arms deal were defeated. Boeing threatened to lay off hundreds of workers if the deal were vetoed. It alone cabled 1600 subcontracting firms urging them to lobby for the sale.[83]

Yet, it was not only those directly benefiting from the proposed deal who were involved. In addition to the many hundreds of major and minor companies – down to small neighborhood workshops – that stood to benefit from the deal, the Saudis and their American friends applied considerable pressure on many other corporations. Whether actual or potential benefactors of Saudi petrodollars, they were urged to join the campaign. Delayed decisions on standing contracts and suggestions of possible future ones were among the instruments of persuasion used by the Saudis in this effort.[84]

A partial list of some 200 of the 700 firms known to have been directly contracted by Saudi Arabia alone (in addition to the many contracted by other Persian Gulf Arab states and to the hundreds of sub-contractors), was published in a Mobil advertisement entitled "Saudi Arabia: For More than Oil."[85] It included the California-based Ralph M. Parsons, Bechtel, and Fluor Corporations – all three contracted for multi-year major construction projects in Saudi Arabia which totaled respectively $10 billion (Yanbu and Jiddah airport); $50 billion (the city of Jubail and Riyadh airport); and $20 billion (a natural gas processing plant and other projects).[86] All three, along with many of the others, were involved in the AWACS campaign. Interestingly, four former employees of one of them – the Bechtel Group Inc. – held or would hold key positions within the Reagan administration. They were Defense Secretary Caspar W. Weinberger, Deputy Energy Secretary W. Kenneth Davis, President Reagan's Special Middle East Envoy Philip C. Haib, and Secretary of State George P. Shultz.

The involvement of the business community with the AWACS issue was the most dramatic manifestation of a new phenomenon. Yet, it was limited neither to exclusively economic issues nor to short-term transactions. A case in point is Mobil Oil's continuing advocacy regarding political dimensions of US Middle East policy. Mobil's support for Riyadh was not to be limited to issues where the financial benefits to the US were obvious. Even such a controversial and seemingly non-economic issue as Prince Fahd's eight-point plan for solving the Arab-Israeli dispute was worthy of Mobil's support as a "good beginning for a lasting peace in the Middle East." Thus Mobil's commitment to the Saudi version of Middle East peace was reponsible for the company's decision to underwrite a series of ads on the subject in most major US papers in the midst of the debate over AWACS.[87]

The growing share of the Arab market in US exports, in both relative and absolute terms, seems to guarantee that the AWACS case will not remain an aberration or an exception in the nature of the involvement of the American business community in influencing US Middle East policies. US exports to the Arab world for the year 1980 totalled $13,200 million. In 1981 they totalled $16,414 million and for 1982 they were estimated to have totalled $20,000 million. The 1982 figure represented an increase of 100% over the 1978 figure, and constituted almost 10% of US exports worldwide.[88]

One of the important manifestations of this very visible lobbying targeted at both the Congress and the general public has been the growing Middle East-related input of the business community into the American electoral process. Between the 1978 and 1980 elections, the money spent by Political Action Committees (PACs) financed by oil interests[89] increased by 111%. This was more than four times the rate of growth in general campaign spending.[90] Concentrating on conservatives – particularly Republicans – oil PACs were successful in helping elect and reelect a significant number of senators and representatives who could not ignore the source for much of their campaign spending. Not surprisingly, in the 97th Congress the four senators who enjoyed oil PACs' major financial efforts were all members of the Senate Finance Committee. Two of them were among Israel's most persistent critics: Steven D. Symms (R: Idaho) and Russell B. Long (D: Louisiana). Equally relevant has been the success of negative lobbying. It contributed to the defeat of a leading proponent of Arab investment disclosures (and a noted supporter of Israel), Senator Frank Church (D: Idaho).[91]

Another manifestation has been repeated public advocacy of pro-Arab policies based on the economic value of the Arab market. Thus, in arguing for less supportive policies toward Israel, one leading member of the pro-Arab lobby organization said: "It amazes me that American companies continue to do business there. I don't know how long Arab patience will last... At some point, because of Israeli behavior, they're going to say 'enough is enough.'"[92] In 1982 a senior State Department official was quoted as having made the same argument in his lecture to a seminar for American businessmen and businesswomen interested in the Middle East.[93] The obvious direct link between the sale of American-made goods on the one hand and jobs for Americans on the other, has thus been expanded to incorporate the suggestion that pro-Arab political stands are essential in order to secure business opportunities for American firms in the Arab world. Thus, for example, on March 3, 1983, while addressing 150 businessmen assembled by the American-Arab Affairs Council (AAAC), former US ambassadors to Saudi Arabia John West and James Akins predicted a total loss of US influence and business opportunities in the Arab world unless the US brought pressure on Israel to withdraw from Lebanon and alter its West Bank policies.[94] The growing number of American executives who argue that "unless we do something constructive on an Arab-Israeli settlement, things are going to get a lot tougher in the years ahead for US firms"[95] may testify to the effectiveness of this line of reasoning.

C. Conclusion and Policy Relevancy

By the end of the "decade of OPEC" most American experts appeared relieved of what, for some, had been their main concern only months earlier: a politically-motivated oil embargo devastating the American economy. This sense of relief derived from recognition of the diminishing share of OAPEC petroleum in total US energy consumption as well as the perception of a fundamental structural change having taken place in the world energy market. Similarly, another presumed tie-in between energy and politics — the direct linkage between developments in the Arab-Israel context and Persian Gulf stability — was also being reassessed. It gave way to a better understanding of more obvious and imminent sources of Persian Gulf regional instability that originate primarily in the domestic context of oil-producing states and in their relations with each other, as well as with Soviet ambitions in this region. The Iran-Iraq War, as well as local incidents that served as reminders of the vulnerability of the present order in several oil-producing Gulf states, taken together with the Soviet invasion of Afghanistan, demonstrated one side of this coin: the intra-Gulf and global contexts of perceived threats.[96] Restrained Arab reaction to the war in Lebanon and the fact that the war did not spill over beyond the Lebanese arena, served to demonstrate the other: the limited relevance of the Arab-Israel arena to Persian Gulf realities.

However, toward the mid-1980s these conclusions and the relief they generated had yet to permeate overall public attitudes. Memories of a decade of politically-motivated threats of, and actual interruptions in, the supply of increasingly expensive oil, died hard. Moreover, the threat of an involuntary interruption, caused either by natural disaster or by intra- or inter-state hostilities, continues to trouble experts and laymen alike. The former generates support for policies geared to increasing US energy independence. The latter, while not directly linked to the Arab-Israeli context,[97] serves to shape American security policies vis-à-vis the Persian Gulf and thus, however indirectly, affects Israeli security.[98]

Consequently, in the era of Selective Interventionism, most Americans no longer expect to solve Persian Gulf problems by forcing Israeli concessions on the question of Palestinian self-determination. Indeed, the notion that any such development might enhance stability in the Gulf has been replaced with an active search for adequate means for adapting to a state of permanent instability. Support for decreasing US dependence is accompanied by the recognition that, even if it eventually is achieved, America's trade partners in Western Europe and Japan are unlikely to enjoy similar freedom from dependence on Gulf oil. Consequently, many Americans seem to support the creation of an independent American capability to deter and, if need be, meet threats to the flow of oil with adequate force to ensure continued access. They expect Western Europe and Japan to make meaningful contributions to this effort. The cooperation of regional allies in this task is also sought.

The implications of this reality to Israeli security are dealt with elsewhere in this study.[99] Meanwhile another dimension of the "decade of OPEC" – the petrodollars phenomenon – caused the reemergence of a direct link between economic prosperity in the US and Washington's policy in the Arab-Israel context. The catalysts have been the perceived consequences of decisions made by members of OAPEC concerning (1) petrodollar investments in the American economy and (2) opportunities for American economic ventures in the OAPEC economies. In both areas, the dual instruments of threats of withdrawals and promises of new investments and contracts have prompted many sectors of the American economy to mobilize on behalf of issues dear to key OAPEC members.

By the early 1980s, what had been tentative, hesitant, low-profile and sporadic lobbying gave way to determined, aggressive and well-coordinated efforts. The targets of these companies were no longer specific administration decisions; their more ambitious objectives now included the reshaping of the cultural, political and military dimensions of public perceptions of Arabs and Israelis, thus affecting the general course and character of US Middle East policy.

This desire to satisfy OAPEC expectations has prompted the American business community to offer generous financial support to (1) educational programs geared to achieve these objectives in both the media and institutes of learning; (2) election campaigns of individuals who support these objectives or who may defeat those opposed to them; and (3) ad-hoc campaigns on behalf of specific policy-decisions. By its growing involvement in underwriting, coordinating and executing these lobbying efforts, the business community has emerged as a potent actor in affecting both short-term and long-term policies and attitudes toward issues relevant to Israeli security. Both financially and organizationally, this new reality presents Israel and pro-Israel lobbies in the US with an awesome challenge. Throughout the 1980s they are likely to have ample opportunity to demonstrate their ability to compete.

Conclusion: The Domestic Setting — Implications for Relations with Israel

Toward the end of the 1970s, and much more intensely and visibly during the early 1980s, many Americans perceived US-Israel relations to be progressing along two seemingly conflicting tracks:

1. increasing Israeli dependence on American contributions — economic, military and political; concurrent with

2. more frequent and independent Israeli initiatives, primarily military but also political, at times in defiance of American preferences.

The frequency of occurrences within the latter category diverted attention for prolonged periods of time from areas of basic agreement, cooperation and affinity, and focused it on the disagreeable. This atmosphere of repeated friction and disagreement accelerated a previously slow process of change in the basic determinants of American attitudes and policies toward Israel. However, by the mid-1980s, while the trends could be readily detected, they had not yet reached fruition or converged to produce a new or less hospitable setting for the formulation of American policies that affect Israeli security.

The general context of these developments has been the current phase of the gradually evaporating "Vietnam syndrome." While hardly a thing of the past, US reluctance to conduct active foreign and security policies in remote areas of the globe has recently been muted. It has given way to a somewhat less isolationist mood defined here as Selective Interventionism. Yet, this mandate for a more assertive external policy, and accompanying public support for the investment in the creation of the instruments of military power, is still a most restricted one. It implies neither *a priori* approval of the actual use of American troops, nor a guarantee for continued support of ever-increasing defense expenditures. Moreover, harsh economic realities at home have already produced a tightfisted approach toward foreign aid. Concurrently, growing impatience with perceived unfriendly attitudes or uncooperative conduct by recipients of this aid — as well as with allies who enjoy the benefits of this new American mood but fail to make their own contribution, financial, political or otherwise, to the assumed common effort – has given rise to explicit demands for more convincing reciprocal contributions.

These general trends threaten to coincide with more basic changes in attitudes toward Israel's disproportionate share of Washington's attention – as well as its finite economic, military and political resources – to produce occasional support for policies less compatible with basic Israeli needs.

The primary cause for these changes has been the inevitable process of the changing of the guard in American politics. With the political maturing of the post-World War II generation, the two dominant filters that served to shape American perceptions of, and thus attitudes toward, Israel – the destruction of European Jewry and the rebirth of Jewish statehood in Palestine – have been losing their potency. The new generation shares neither the sense of guilt toward the victims of the Holocaust, nor the vivid memories of Israel's pioneering beginning and courageous emergence that revolutionized Jewish existence in a uniquely successful experiment in democratic national reconstruction. This generation's sympathies are determined by current, rather than historical, images. And these, in turn, are determined by present judgments of value affinity and moral conduct accompanied by assessments of contribution to American interests.

By the mid-1980s, in the wake of a most trying period, Israel still ranked high on both counts among the US public-at-large as well as in the US Congress. Although the specific weight of its powerful advocates in Congress was declining and the American Jewish community itself was undergoing a socio-demographic transformation that threatened to erode its political influence, these processes were sufficiently slow in maturing to promise that the impending change would not be abrupt. Consequently, at the time of writing, as perceptions of the older and younger generations mix to produce popular inputs into the policymaking process, Israel still enjoys broad-based sympathy. Translated into the unusual popularity of generous American aid – economic and military – that sympathy encompasses broad support for specific Israeli stands within the Arab-Israel peace process. Yet, even at this transitory stage, America's support is neither unrestricted nor unconditional.

Clearly, Israel is hardly relevant to the shaping and relative weight of some of the limitations on this support. Most obviously, the rates of economic growth and unemployment in the US and the changing global energy and monetary markets have nothing to do with Israel's conduct. Yet Jerusalem can hardly hope to escape the consequences of these seemingly unrelated trends. The political cost of staggering budget deficits and further cuts in welfare programs may force future administrations to curtail expenditures in two areas of importance to Israel: foreign aid and defense.

With regard to the former, by the second half of the 1980s anything short of a continued sustained increase in allocations and rescheduling or canceling of debt, will translate into declining net economic aid (i.e., total aid less repayment of interest and principal) to Israel. Military aid, meant to enable Israel to sustain a reasonable military balance with its potential adversaries, may have to be increased as well. Both the rapidly increasing cost of weapons systems and the maturity of expansion and modernization efforts of armed forces in several Arab states may accentuate that need in the very near future.

As to the latter, if sustained, increased investment in conventional forces and force projection capabilities holds the promise of continued American ability to provide Israel with newer generations of military technology and to undertake the necessary steps to protect western interests in the Middle East, respectively. While in the long run the potential emergence of an independent American capacity for adequate force projection may obviate present dependence on the cooperation of potent regional allies, at the time of writing such an eventuality seems rather remote.

On the other hand, economic realities are expected to yield significant restrictions on the Pentagon budget, particularly of the kind that may revive the tendency toward concentrated investment in nuclear capabilities at the expense of R&D and procurement of conventional weapons systems. Such a course of events will present Israel with the economically unfeasible task of augmenting American efforts with efforts of its own to develop self-sufficiency in an increasing number of first line major weapons systems.

Consequently, by the late 1980s Israel may be faced with the coincidence of a declining net American aid with a sharp increase in the burden of defense expenditures. Both, while hardly divorced from Israel's perceived conduct, are primarily by-products of developments beyond Israel's control.

Perceptions of American dependence on OAPEC-produced petroleum and the reality of the growing influence of petrodollars on the American political scene constitute another potential restriction on American generosity with regard to Israel. On the one hand, it appears as though the general public is gradually accepting both the limited relevance of the Arab-Israel conflict to the flow of Persian Gulf oil and its price, as well as the evaporating potency of oil boycotts for political purposes. On the other hand, as long as OAPEC revenues and reserves constitute significant sources of currency-injections into the American economy – through either investments or purchases of goods and services – the American business community may be expected to continue to demonstrate its recently acquired incentive and capability to lobby effectively on behalf of causes dear to members of OAPEC. Support for Israel will continue to be the obvious target of such negative campaigns.

In addition to such uncontrollable elements (from the Israeli standpoint), America's support is also conditional on variables that are well within Israel's control. Jerusalem's ability to project an unbending commitment to peace, and its success in convincing Americans that its resort to force is restricted exclusively to measures justified by legitimate security considerations, are the two most relevant examples. In recent years the American public and Congress have demonstrated growing willingness to see Israel punished whenever its conduct was judged to exceed its legitimate security needs. This trend is likely to intensify in the future.

Similarly, while Americans seem consistently not to qualify their unconditional support for Israel's national existence, their support for Israel's definition of security in territorial terms and for other basic Israeli positions within the Arab-Israel conflict *is* conditional. It draws on broad-based perceptions of a firm Israeli commitment to the peaceful resolution of the conflict, based on the territories-for-peace formula. Significantly, here, too, Israel is not the sole master of its destiny. Some Israeli policies do raise doubts about the sincerity of Israel's willingness to withdraw from territories occupied in 1967 in order to facilitate a peaceful accommodation, thereby undermining congressional and public support. Yet, not only Jerusalem can alter American attitudes. An Arab peace initiative that convinces Americans of its sincerity could be equally potent in reversing the otherwise firm support for basic Israeli pre-negotiation positions. Indeed, an Arab gesture that involves a publicly stated unequivocal commitment to peaceful accommodation, could hold the promise of American public and legislative support for major arms purchases, nothwithstanding Israel's growing concern with the cumulative impact of this trend on regional military balances in the later 1980s.

Consequently, those charged with the primary responsibility for formulating and executing relevant American policies in the late 1980s are presented with a complex mandate.

- They are expected to produce Arab concessions within the Arab-Israel peace process, but have limited leverage over them and are faced with a potent, pro-Arab business lobby at home.
- They are expected to produce Israeli concessions within the Arab-Israel peace process, but are restricted in pressuring Israel to instances when the American public and Congress are convinced that Israel alone is to blame for lack of progress. In the absence of an Arab partner this is a most difficult task.
- They are expected to act firmly when American interests in this region are threatened, but neither have at their disposal adequate independent means, nor are authorized in advance to use whatever force is available for that purpose.
- They are expected to augment US capabilities with those of friendly allies from the region, but are faced with the potential adverse consequences to the peace process of providing these allies with the military means necessary for their contribution to the common objective.

In sum, it appears that from the mid-1980s to the end of the decade, any administration in Washington will be faced with a changing domestic context for its Middle East policies.

The unconditional and irreversible realities – hence, firm basis for support – of the debt to the survivors of the Holocaust and admiration for Israel's pioneering spirit, have gradually given way to more conditional and potentially transitory, hence more vulnerable, premises of support for Israel. These emerging new major determinants of the *will* of legislators and their constituencies to launch major political battles on behalf of Israel or, conversely, to tolerate or even demand punitive measures against it, are Israel's perceived contribution to American interests and, equally weighty, the perceived righteousness of its objectives, policies and instruments of implementation. Increasingly, too, the capacity of the American public and its representatives in Washington to shield Israel from punishment or impose measures favorable to Jerusalem will be affected by economic realities at home. As suggested above, throughout a most trying decade these "dams" demonstrated their durability. This durability, however, should not be mistaken for invulnerability. One thing is certain: American willingness to continue fulfilling this crucial protective role will be determined increasingly by Israel's own conduct.

Appendices

Appendix A

US MILITARY AND ECONOMIC AID TO ISRAEL: 1948-1983

(current $million)

FY	Economic Assistance			Military Aid			Total Aid			Relevant Political/Military Developments
	Loans	Grants	Total	Loans	Grants	Total	Loans	Grants	Total	
1948	-	-	-	-	-	-	-	-	-	
1949	-	-	-	-	-	-	-	-	-	
1950	-	-	-	-	-	-	-	-	-	
1951	-	0.1	0.1	-	-	-	-	0.1	0.1	
1952	-	86.4	86.4	-	-	-	-	86.4	86.4	
1953	-	73.6	73.6	-	-	-	-	73.6	73.6	
1954	-	74.7	74.7	-	-	-	-	74.7	74.7	
1955	30.8	21.9	52.7	-	-	-	30.8	21.9	52.7	
1956	35.2	15.6	50.8	-	-	-	35.2	15.6	50.8	
1957	21.8	19.1	40.9	-	-	-	21.8	19.1	40.9	
1958	49.9	11.3	61.2	-	-	-	49.9	11.3	61.2	
1959	39.2	10.9	49.9	0.4	-	0.4	39.4	10.9	50.3	
1960	41.8	13.4	55.2	0.5	-	0.5	42.3	13.4	55.7	
1961	29.8	18.3	48.1	-	-	-	29.8	18.3	48.1	
1962	63.5	7.2	70.7	13.2	-	13.2	76.7	7.2	83.9	
1963	57.4	6.0	63.4	13.3	-	13.3	70.7	6.0	76.7	
1964	32.2	4.8	37.0	-	-	-	32.2	4.8	37.0	
1965	43.9	4.9	48.8	12.9	-	12.9	56.8	4.9	61.7	

(cont. on next pg.)

143

(cont. from previous pg.)

FY	Economic Assistance			Military Aid			Total Aid			Relevant Political/Military Developments
	Loans	Grants	Total	Loans	Grants	Total	Loans	Grants	Total	
1966	35.9	0.9	36.8	90.0	-	90.0	125.9	0.9	126.8	
1967	75.5	0.6	76.1	7.0	-	7.0	82.5	0.6	83.1	
1968	51.3	0.5	51.8	25.0	-	25.0	76.3	0.5	76.8	
1969	36.1	0.6	36.7	85.0	-	85.0	121.1	0.6	121.7	
1970	40.7	0.4	41.1	30.0	-	30.0	70.7	0.4	71.1	
1971	55.5	0.3	55.8	545.0	-	545.0	600.5	0.3	600.8	1. The Rogers Plan. 2. US-Israel cooperation against Syrian invasion of Jordan.
1972	53.8	50.4	104.2	300.0	-	300.0	353.8	50.4	404.2	
1973	59.4	50.4	109.8	300.0	-	300.0	359.4	50.4	409.8	
1974	-	51.4	51.4	980.0	1,600.0	2,580.0	980.0	1,651.4	2,631.4	Post-Yom Kippur War aid package.
1975	8.6	344.5	353.1	200.0	100.0	300.0	208.6	444.5	653.1	
1976	239.4	475.0	714.4	850.0	850.0	1,700.0	1,089.4	1,325.0	2,414.4	Aid related to 2nd Israel-Egypt interim agreement.
1977	245.0	490.0	735.0	500.0	500.0	1,000.0	745.0	990.0	1,735.0	
1978	260.8	525.0	785.0	500.0	500.0	1,000.0	760.0	1,025.0	1,791.8	
1979	260.0	525.0	785.0	2,700.0	600.0	3,300.0	2,960.0	1,125.0	4,085.0	Including Camp David-related aid package.

(cont. on next pg.)

144

(cont. from previous pg.)

FY	Economic Assistance			Military Aid			Total Aid			Relevant Political/Military Developments
	Loans	Grants	Total	Loans	Grants	Total	Loans	Grants	Total	
1980	260.0	525.0	785.0	500.0	500.0	1,000.0	760.0	1,025.0	1,785.0	
1981	-	764.0	764.0	900.0	500.0	1,400.0	900.0	1,264.0	2,164.0	
1982	-	806.0	806.0	850.0	550.0	1,400.0	850.0	1,356.0	2,206.0	
1983	-	785.0	785.0	950.0	750.0	1,700	950.0	1,535.0	2,485.0	
TOTAL	2126.7	5763.2	7889.7	10,352.3	6,450.0	16,802.3	12,478.8	12,213.2	24,692.0	

Sources: 1948-1966: Davar, October 12, 1982.
1967-1971: Based on Paul Rivlin, "The Burden of Israel's Defense," Survival, vol. xx, no. 4 (July/August 1978), p. 148.
1972-1983: Comptroller General of the US, US Assistance to State of Israel (Washington, DC: GAO) June 24, 1983, pp. 8, 30.

145

Appendix B.

<u>FLOW CHART OF US FOREIGN AID LEGISLATION</u>

1. Authorization

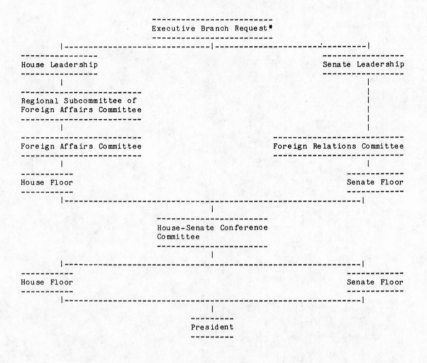

Source: Based on <u>The US Congress: A Guide to Citizen Action</u> (Washington, DC:
AIPAC, May 1983).

*Commonly submitted in February for the following fiscal year, that begins
October 1.

146

2. Appropriation*

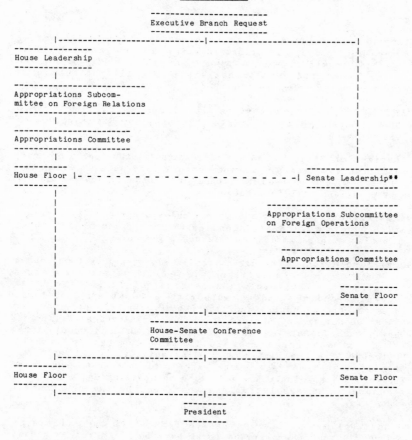

```
                    -------------------------
                    Executive Branch Request
                    -------------------------
    |------------------------------|------------------------------|
----------------                                                  |
House Leadership                                                  |
----------------                                                  |
        |                                                         |
-----------------------------                                     |
Appropriations Subcom-                                            |
mittee on Foreign Relations                                       |
-----------------------------                                     |
        |                                                         |
---------------------------                                       |
Appropriations Committee                                          |
---------------------------                                       |
        |                                         ---------------------
-----------                                       Senate Leadership**
House Floor |- - - - - - - - - - - - - - - - - -| ---------------------
-----------                                               |
        |                                         ----------------------------
        |                                         Appropriations Subcommittee
        |                                         on Foreign Operations
        |                                         ----------------------------
        |                                                 |
        |                                         ---------------------------
        |                                         Appropriations Committee
        |                                         ---------------------------
        |                                                 |
        |                                           ------------
        |                                           Senate Floor
        |                                           ------------
    |------------------------------|------------------------------|
                    -------------------------
                    House-Senate Conference
                    Committee
                    -------------------------
    |------------------------------|------------------------------|
-----------                                               ------------
House Floor                                               Senate Floor
-----------                                               ------------
    |------------------------------|------------------------------|
                        ----------
                        President
                        ----------
```

---

*Appropriation bill deliberations are based on actual or projected figures of authorization.

**Traditionally, Senate deliberations follow conclusion of House action.

Appropriations Bill. An act of Congress that grants the actual monies approved by authorization bills, but not necessarily to the total permissible under the authorization bill. Originates in the House, and usually not acted on until the companion authorization measure is passed.

ARAMCO. The Arabian American Oil Company. Oil consortium consisting of Mobil Oil, Exxon, Texaco, and Standard Oil of California.

Authorization Bill. An act of Congress that authorizes a program, specifies its general aim and conduct, and puts a ceiling on monies that can be used to finance it. Usually enacted before appropriations bill is passed.

Budget Authority. Funds authorized and appropriated by Congress which permit government agencies to enter into obligations, requiring either immediate or future payments.

Budget Resolution. A concurrent resolution passed by both houses of Congress which establishes the federal budget for a given fiscal year. The resolution sets target levels for total federal spending (budget authority and outlays), federal revenues, and an estimate of the public debt. It provides for budget authority and outlays for 19 different budget functions. During each fiscal year Congress passes two such resolutions. The first concurrent resolution is expected to pass by September 15. The latter is binding and revises or reaffirms the functional and aggregate targets of the first resolution. The resolution establishes a ceiling on spending and a floor on revenues. The resolution does not require the president's signature.

Constant Dollars. Dollar estimates from which the effects of changes in the general price level have been removed, reported in terms of a base year value.

Continuing Resolution (Stoppage Resolution). A joint resolution of both houses of Congress meant to continue appropriations at rates based on those of the previous FY.

Current Dollars. Dollar values that have not been corrected for changes in the general price level.

Decontrol. Removal of government-imposed price controls so that market forces determine the price of a commodity.

Deferral. Impoundment by the president that delays the expenditure of funds appropriated by the Congress.

Earmark. Specifying funds for a particular purpose. Commonly used in order to impose congressional preferences in funding specific programs within broader budget categories.

ESF. Economic Support Funds. US government-financed loans and grants.

Expenditures (or outlays). The actual disbursement of funds during a given FY. Commonly represents funds appropriated also in previous years.

FMS. Foreign Military Sales. US government-guaranteed loans. Not included as new budget authority. Meant to enable the recipient to obtain loans in the American financial market for the purpose of purchasing US-made military equipment.

Function 150. One of nineteen different budget functions included in congressional budget resolutions. Function 150 covers international affairs, and includes the entire Foreign Assistance Program.

FY. Fiscal year. Runs from October 1 through September 30.

IMET. International Military Education and Training. US government-funded military education and training programs either in the US or in the recipient country.

Impoundment. Presidential action to delay, reduce or terminate the expenditure of funds appropriated by the Congress.

Markup. Committee meeting(s) held after hearings are completed, for the purpose of amending, revising or tabling a bill.

MAP. Military Assistance Program. US government grants for the purpose of purchasing US-made military equipment.

MBD. Million Barrels per Day. An international measure of oil trade and production. One MBD equals 48.9 metric tons of oil per year. Each metric ton of oil contains 7.33 barrels.

OAPEC. Organization of Arab Petroleum Exporting Countries. Comprises Algeria, Bahrain, Libya, Neutral Zone, Qatar, Saudi Arabia, Syria, United Arab Emirates, and Tunisia. In 1979 Egypt was suspended from OAPEC. Syria, Egypt, Bahrain, and Tunisia are not members of OPEC.

Outlays. See **Expenditures.**

Recision. Impoundment by the president that terminates or cuts the expenditure of funds appropriated by the Congress.

Report. v. The act of returning a bill by a committee to the floor of the House. n. The document that sets forth a committee's explanations of its action on a bill.

Resolution of Disapproval. A concurrent resolution to block the transfer of US military equipment or services exceeding $25 million, or a single major military item exceeding $7 million, to any foreign country. Under Section 36(b) of the Arms Export Control Act, the president must send to the Congress formal notification of his intention to make any such sale. The notice is referred to the Senate Foreign Relations and House Foreign Affairs committees for initial consideration. The letter of offer shall not be issued if the Senate and House, within 30 calendar days after receiving such certification, adopt the resolution stating that they object to the proposed sale. If either the Senate or House fails to take action, the arms sale would proceed. A resolution of disapproval is not subject to a presidential veto.

SPR. Strategic Petroleum Reserve. Authorized by the Congress in 1975 in order to provide a security element in the case of major supply disruptions.

Stopgap Resolution. See **Continuing Resolution.**

Supplemental Appropriations. Additional funds appropriated by Congress for current FY. Intended to cover expenses that exceed those specified in the regular appropriations bills.

Table. A motion to defer consideration of a bill. Usually used to suspend all further deliberations, thus killing the measure.

TOA. Total Obligational Authority. Represents commitments to programs, payments for which come due in phased fashion over several fiscal years.

Veto. Disapproval by the president of a bill or joint resolution.

NOTES

Introduction

1   Harvey S. Sicherman, "The United States and Israel: A Strategic Divide?" *Orbis* 24, no. 2 (Summer 1980): 1.

2   Organization of Arab Petroleum Exporting Countries.

3   Graham Allison, *Essence of Decision* (Boston: Little, Brown, 1971); Alexander L. George, "The Case for Multiple Advocacy in Making Foreign Policy," *American Political Science Review*, vol. 66, no. 3 (September 1972); I.M. Destler, *Presidents, Bureaucrats, and Foreign Policy* (Princeton University Press, 1972); and Morton Halperin, *Bureaucratic Politics and Foreign Policy* (Washington: Brookings Institution, 1974).

4   See John Spanier and Eric M. Uslaner, *How American Foreign Policy is Made* (New York: Holt, Rinehart and Winston, 1978).

5   Interestingly, in 1975 a panel of eight leading public opinion researchers concluded that the American public wished "the Congress to take a stronger part in overseeing the activities of the executive branch" specifically in foreign policy. "Polsters Report of Foreign Policy," *Congressional Record-Senate*, October 8, 1975, p. S17770.

6   Noting important exceptions, particularly since 1965, this basic argument is generally supported even by studies amplifying issue-areas where congressional involvement is noticeable. See, for example, Randall B. Ripley, *Congress: Process and Policy* (New York: W.W. Norton & Co., 1978). See also David M. Abshire and Ralph D. Nurnberger (eds.), *The Growing Power of Congress* (Sage for CSIS, 1981).

7   William B. Quandt, *Decade of Decisions: American Policy Toward the Arab-Israeli Conflict* (Los Angeles: University of California Press, 1977), p. 22; William B. Quandt, "Domestic Influences on US Foreign Policy in the Middle East: The View from Washington" in Willard A. Beling (ed.), *The Middle East: Quest for an American Policy* (Albany: State University of New York, 1973), pp. 274-75, 281-82; Marvin Feuerwerger, *Congress and Israel: Foreign Aid Decision-Making in the House of Representatives 1969-1976* (Connecticut: Greenwood Press, 1979). For a prediction that "Congressional involvement will mark the largest single difference between American foreign policy-making in the last quarter of this century and that of the preceding decades" see Graham Allison and Peter Szanton, *Remaking Foreign Policy: The Organizational Connection* (New York: Basic Books, 1976). Quote from p. 99 See also, Richard Haas, *Congressional Power: Implications for American Security Policy* (Adelphi Papers, No. 153, IISS: London, 1979). For the opposite view, see Abshire and Nurnberger (eds.), *The Growing Power of Congress*.

8   Ronald C. Moe and Steven C. Teel, "Congress as Policy-Maker: A Necessary Reappraisal," *Political Science Quarterly* 85 (1970): 49.

9   Ripley, *Congress: Process and Policy*, pp. 381-385.

10   A process documented, for example, in Richard F. Fenno Jr., *Congressmen in Committee* (Boston: Little, Brown & Co., 1973). See also, Eric L. Davis, "The President and Congress," in Arnold J. Meltsner (ed.), *Politics and the Oval Office* (San Francisco: Inst. for Contemporary Studies, 1981), pp. 103-121.

11   Holbert N. Carrol, *The House of Representatives and Foreign Affairs* (Pittsburgh: University of Pittsburgh Press, 1966), p. 12. See also, Quandt, *Decade of Decisions*, p. 15.

12   On the power to persuade, see Richard E. Neustadt, *Presidential Power: The Politics of Leadership from FDR to Carter* (New York: John Wiley, 1980). On the political utility of public opinion, see Richard C. Cohen, *The Public's Impact on Foreign Policy* (Boston: Little, Brown & Co., 1973).

13   William B. Quandt, *Decade of Decisions*, pp. 15-17. See also, George Gallup Jr.'s assessment in "Polsters' Report," p. S17772. For a conflicting view, representing the school of thought that argues that public opinion tends to confirm rather than constrain government actions, see Robert Weissberg, *Public Opinion and Popular Government* (Englewood Cliffs, NJ: Prentice Hall, 1976).

14   On the volatile character of public opinion concerning foreign and security matters, see Gabriel Almond, *The American People and Foreign Policy* (New York: Praeger, 1960). For a markedly different conclusion see Benjamin I. Page and Robert Y. Shapiro, "Changes in Americans' Policy Preferences, 1935-1979," *Public Opinion Quarterly*, vol. 46, no. 1 (Spring, 1982), pp. 24-42.

15   As demonstrated in Chapter I below. See also, Quandt, *Decade of Decisions*, p. 18, and Seymour Martin Lipset, "Further Commentary on American Attitudes," *Public Opinion*, vol. 1, no. 2 (May/June 1978), pp. 16-17.

16   William B. Quandt, "Domestic Influences," p. 282. See also, Robert H. Trice, "Foreign Policy Interest Groups, Mass Public Opinion and the Arab-Israeli Dispute," *Western Political Quarterly*, vol. 31, no. 2 (June 1978), pp. 238-252.

17   As quoted in Seymour Martin Lipset, "Further Commentary," p. 16.

18   This apathy was explained by James Zogby, executive director of the American-Arab Anti-Discrimination Committee, in the following words: "To be frank about Arab-Americans, if it is a difference between two candidates who won't address the issues they're concerned about, they're not going to vote." *Los Angeles Herald Examiner*, February 5, 1984.

19   *Ibid.*

20   In late 1979 a Gallup poll found that only 5% of American Blacks expressed any interest in the Middle East. *Newsweek*, September 3, 1979.

21   For one discussion of the operational environment as a useful concept for foreign policy decisionmaking analysis, see Michael Brecher, Belma Steinberg and Janice Stein, "A Framework for Research on Foreign Policy Behavior," *Journal of Conflict Resolution*, XIII, no. 1 (1969), pp. 75-101. Brecher utilized this concept, *inter alia*, in his *Decisions in Israel's Foreign Policy* (New Haven, Conn: Yale University Press, 1975).

22   For an argument on the link between the defense budget on the one hand and US deterrence, research and development (R&D) and resupply capabilities on the other, see Edward N. Luttwak, *Strategy and Politics* (New Brunswick, NJ: Transaction Books, 1980), pp. 141-160. On the lessons of the 1973 War concerning public attitudes toward this linkage, see Feuerwerger, *Congress and Israel*, pp. 134-136.

Chapter 1

1   As quoted in *National Journal*, May 2, 1981, p. 779. This was the first time a president addressed the group, composed of the principal conservative organizations in the USA.

2   William Watt and Lloyd Free, "Nationalism Not Isolationism," *Foreign Policy*, Fall 1976, pp. 3-26. See also "Polsters Report of Foreign Policy," *Congressional Record-Senate*, October 8, 1975, pp. S1770-S1775.

3   *Public Opinion*, February/March 1980, p. 13. 53% favored a more aggressive US policy; 30% opposed it.

4   56% of those questioned in late 1978. *Ibid.*

5   44% of those questioned in late 1978. *Ibid.*

6   58% of those questioned in late 1978. *Ibid.*

7   55% of those questioned in late 1978. This was an increase of 22%, since 33% of those questioned in 1974 shared that sentiment. *Ibid.*

8   In 1977 the Gallup Organization found 40% of the public supportive of the draft. This number rose to 49% in the spring of 1979. *Ibid.*

9   Public support for CIA activities rose from 43% in 1974 to 59% in 1978. Gallup findings as quoted in John Rielly, "The American Mood: A Foreign Policy of Self-Interest," *Foreign Policy*, #34 (Spring, 1979), p. 80.

10   Public support for the use of force, however, was limited to very few instances. Thus, for example, in 1974 39% of those questioned supported the use of force in response to a Soviet invasion of Western Europe. By July 1978 that figure rose to 43%. Four months later, 54% held that view. See: *Public Opinion*, February-March 1980, p. 131.

11   *International Herald Tribune* (IHT), February 23, 1981. Similar findings are reported by the Chicago Council on Foreign Relations in its *American Public Opinion and US Foreign Policy*, (Chicago, Ill, 1980) where the figures for February 1980 and October 1979 were 44% and 6% respectively. The previous time that foreign issues were judged more important than domestic issues was in 1972, during an acute phase of the Vietnam War.

12   A Gallup Organization finding of January 1980. *Public Opinion*.

13   *Ibid.* According to Yankelovitz., Skelly & White, Inc., the ratio was 57:40 in favor of the draft. *Time*, February 11, 1980.

14   Views in relation to "setting up a system of Selective Service Registration to be able to go to a military draft in an emergency." NBC/Louis Harris poll as reported by *Los Angeles Herald Examiner*, February 14, 1980. According to Yankelevitz, *et al.*, the ratio was 73:6. *Time*, February 11, 1980.

15   ABC/Louis Harris poll, as reported in *Public Opinion*.

16   AP/NBC poll, *Public Opinion*.

17   See Gallup poll, as reported in *National Journal*, January 9, 1982, p. 58.

18   *Time*, June 1, 1981.

19   Daniel Yankelovitz and Larry Keegan, "Assertive America," *Foreign Affairs*, vol. 59, no. 3, pp. 696-713.

20   CBS/*New York Times* poll asked in June 1979 and again in January 1980 whether the United States was "superior in military strength to the Soviet Union," about equal, or not as strong. Both queries produced similar results: 43-44% said that the Soviet Union was superior and 11-14% felt that the US was stronger. *Opinion Outlook*, December 8, 1980, pp. 5-6. The same assessment was expressed in

a 1981 poll where 40% felt the Soviets were superior while 15% thought the US was. Richman, "Public Attitudes." See also Nincik and Russett, p. 394. By 1983 13% felt the US was stronger; 38% still thought it was weaker. *National Journal*, September 10, 1983, p. 1862. For a similar assessment of the public mood, see I.M. Destler, "Reagan and Congress – Lessons of 1981," *Washington Quarterly*, Spring 1982, p. 4.

21   For a similar assessment see the conclusion by I.A. Lewis that accompanied his July 1982 *Times* poll: "What Americans say they want is a tough foreign policy based on a strong military that the government, nonetheless, should be reluctant to use." *Los Angeles Times*, July 13, 1982.

22   Compare with Richman, "Public Attitudes," p. 45. See also Bruce Russett and Donald R. Deluca, "Don't Tread on Me: Public Opinion and Foreign Policy in the Eighties," *Political Science Quarterly*, vol. 96, no. 3 (Fall, 1981),pp. 381-399, as well as Miroslav Nincic and Bruce Russett, "The Effect of Similarity and Interest on Attitudes toward Foreign Countries," *Public Opinion Quarterly*, 33 (Spring, 1979): 68-78. For an early detection of this phase, see "Pollsters Report," particularly excerpts from statement by Daniel Yankelovich, p. S17774.

23   The terms Hardliner and Accommodationist are used by Michael A. Magiotto and Eugene R. Wittkopf in their "American Public Attitudes Toward Foreign Policy," *International Studies Quarterly*, vol. 25, no. 4 (December 1981), pp. 601-631. The figures are from a February 1981 poll taken by Roper and reported in Richman, "Public Attitudes."

24   Ole R. Holsti, "The Three Headed Eagle: The United States and System Change," *International Studies Quarterly*, vol. 23, no. 3 (September 1979), p. 351.

25   Roper, in Richman, "Public Attitudes."

26   See Introduction above.

27   Roper, in Richman, "Public Attitudes."

28   In 1981 Yankelovitch *et al.* found that 47% of the voters considered themselves conservatives and 13% liberals. A year earlier the distribution was 41:14. *Time*, December 28, 1981, p. 47. Interestingly, the "move to the right," as defined here was not reflected in corresponding changes in party affiliation. *Ibid.*

29   See Rielly, "American Opinion," 1983, Table p. 99.

30   In at least three consecutive *Los Angeles Times* polls, "conservatives gave consistently greater support to Israel...than did those who identified themselves as liberals." *Los Angeles Times*, July 11, 1982. A late June 1982 Harris Poll supported these findings. *Yediot Aharonot*, July 26, 1982.

31   For a discussion of this phenomenon, see, for example, Jack Citrin, "The Changing American Electorate," in Arnold J. Meltsner (ed.), *Politics and the Oval Office* (San Francisco: Institute of Contemporary Studies, 1981), pp. 31-61.

32   Louis Harris polls put support for military action at 79% in April; 71% in September; and 65% just after election day in November. *Opinion Outlook*, December 8, 1980, p. 5.

33   In October 1981, 72% of those polled supported the use of force under such circumstances. The *Washington Post*, October 21, 1981.

34   See Tables I, IV above.

35   Richman, "Public Attitudes." Similar findings were reported by NBC/Harris poll: initial support for the use of military force to protect access to Persian Gulf oil was 69:21. *Los Angeles Herald Examiner*, February 14, 1980.

36   Interestingly, in November 1978 Americans were found more willing to react

by military means to an oil cut-off. See Table I above. By late 1978 Gallup found Americans opposed to the use of force under such circumstances by a ratio of 61:39%. Rielly, "American Opinion," 1983, p. 99.

37   The *Washington Post*, October 21, 1981.

38   Surprisingly, Robert Lichter found 72% of the "national news elite" (editors and writers of the main dailies and weeklies as well as the broadcasting networks) in support of an American military commitment to Israel. Leon Hadar, "Pro-Israel Press," the *Jerusalem Post*, April 25, 1982.

39   Several weeks after the September 17, 1978 conclusion of the Camp David Accords, at 78% Israel was second only to Saudi Arabia (80%) and equal to Japan, although more Americans felt Japan was not important (11%) than those who felt that way about Israel (8%). Egypt – the other Camp David signatory – ranked fifth (75%), ahead of the Soviet Union (74%). Respondents were asked to indicate whether they felt "the US does or does not have a vital interest" in any of twenty-four countries listed. See John E. Rielly, "The American Mood," 1979, p. 83. Interestingly, in late 1981, in answering an identical question but provided with a much shorter list of countries to rank, Israel remained second (at 81%) to Saudi Arabia (84%) with Egypt and Canada considered vital by 78% of the respondents each. The Gallup Organization, as reported in *Attitudes Concerning the American Jewish Community: The Gallup Poll, November 1981* (no author), the American Jewish Committee, December 1981, p. 2. A similar result had been obtained by Roper in February 1979. Then, the question was restricted to three major Middle East actors: Israel was ranked first (84%); Saudi Arabia second (83%); and Egypt third (82%), although more respondents felt Israel and Egypt were not important to US interests (11%) than Saudi Arabia (10%). Richard H. Curtiss, *Changing Image* (Washington, DC: American Educational Trust, 1982), p. 202.

40   In 1979 the Louis Harris organization found just under 80% of those questioned defining Israel as a close ally or friend of the US. This was a 4% increase, since 75% had given the same answer in 1974. Curtiss, *Ibid.*, p. 203.

41   The Louis Harris poll found 86% of those questioned supportive of that statement. *B'nai B'rith Messenger*, October 17, 1980. See also Harris' July findings (81% positive) in *Ha'aretz*, October 3, 1980. An identical proportion had agreed with the same statement in 1975. See William C. Adams, "Middle East Meets West: Surveying American Attitudes," *Public Opinion*, April/May 1982, p. 53.

42   In 1980, 62% supported that statement; 20% rejected it. *B'nai B'rith Messenger*, October 17, 1980.

43   As published in *General Social Surveys 1972-1978: Cumulative Codebook*, General Social Surveys, the National Data Program for the Social Science, at National Opinion Research Center, University of Chicago and Roper Public Opinion Research Center, Yale University, July 1978, p. 85. Their findings for the year 1976 are supported by Louis Harris as well, reporting a 74% positive rating. *Ha'aretz*, October 3, 1980. Gallup's findings for January 1980 were identical. Geraldine Rosenfeld, "Attitudes of the American Public Toward American Jews and Israel: August 1979; March-April 1980" (unpublished report), June 1980, pp. 1-2. In 1981, with the increased saliency of the question of reliability, twice as many Americans regarded Israel as a "reliable ally" as did Saudi Arabia. *Washington Post*, October 21, 1981. For similar findings, see poll by Yankelovich, Skelly and White, Inc., as reported in *Time*, December 28, 1981. In early 1982, a *Washington Post*/ABC News poll also found three out of four Americans to hold a positive image of Israel.

Jerusalem Post, May 5, 1982. Similarly, in late June 1982, in the midst of the Israeli invasion of Lebanon, 79% of those questioned labeled Israel as either "a close ally" or "friend" of the US. This was a 4% increase since 75% had felt that way in January 1982. During the same period the percent of those who did not share this view declined from 17% in January to 13% in late June. Louis Harris Survey, as reported in *Los Angeles Herald Examiner,* July 12, 1982. See also *Near East Report,* XXVI, no. 28 (July 9, 1982), p. 139.

44   *B'nai B'rith Messenger,* October 17, 1980.

45   The figures were – 1977: 50%; September 1981: 57% (and 70% of those who expressed an opinion). Yankelovitz *et al., Jerusalem Post,* September 7, 1981. For similar findings for May 1981, see: AP/NBC News poll, *Los Angeles Herald Examiner,* May 26, 1981. An ABC News/*Washington Post* poll of October 1981 also found 60% support for current or increased levels of aid. Adams, "Middle East Meets West," p. 55. These findings are particularly striking in light of the overwhelming negative attitude toward foreign aid in general (see Table XVII).

46   See discussion below. Less comprehensive evidence can be seen in the findings of a mid-1982 Garth-Furst International – Penn & Schoen Associates poll. Asked to choose between Israel and Saudi Arabia as an ally, 62% said it should be Israel (up from 58% in August 1981) and 23% chose Saudi Arabia (down from 27%). *Los Angeles Herald Examiner,* May 21, 1982.

47   See CBS/*New York Times* poll as reported in the *New York Times,* November 7, 1977. It appears that the potential threat to their own well-being compelled a sizable portion of those with "No opinion" to take a stand.

48   See, for example, Shelly Slade, "The Image of the Arab in America," p. 156; Adams, "Middle East Meets West," p. 54; Louis Harris poll, in *Yediot Aharonot,* July 26, 1982.

49   *Washington Post*/ABC poll, in *International Herald Tribune,* August 24, 1982.

50   Reporting his findings in a mid-1982 poll, David Garth concluded: "What is most interesting is that during a period of heavy press reports from Israel, and increased strain between Washington and Israel, there appears to be no erosion of support for Israel. On the contrary, since August 1981...the American public has increased its support for Israel and continues to view Israel as America's best friend in the Middle East." *ADL Bulletin,* June 1982, p. 1. See also, *Los Angeles Herald Examiner,* May 21, 1982.

51   *Washington Post*/ABC poll, in *International Herald Tribune,* August 24, 1982.

52   One study, for example, found that exposure to Watergate-related television had no discernible impact on attitudes toward Nixon for high interest individuals. Thomas A. Kazee, "Television Exposure and Attitude Change: The Impact of Political Interest." *Public Opinion Quarterly,* vol. 1, no. 4 (Winter 1981), pp. 507-518. For a comprehensive list of studies that reached the same conclusion, see *Ibid.,* p. 516.

53   As early as the mid-1970s, S.M. Lipset and Everett Ladd, in their survey of American professors, found a negative correlation between the degree of one's liberalism and support for Israel. For the findings and their analysis see Seymour Martin Lipset and William Schneider, *American Opinion Towards Israel and Jews* (unpublished monograph, n.d.), pp. 40-41.

54   68% supported this statement; 23% opposed. Louis Harris poll as reported by the *Jerusalem Post,* July 22, 1982.

55   "Right" here refers to our earlier definition of the "turn to the right" in section

A above. The data is from Harris poll, *Ibid.* See also fn. 30 above.

56   A 44:37% plurality was found to feel that way in July 1980. Louis Harris poll as reported in *Ha'aretz* and *Yediot Aharonot,* October 3, 1980. See also *B'nai B'rith Messenger,* October 17, 1980. Phrased less dramatically, in 1978 36% of respondents supported American pressure on Israel in the context of the peace process. 57% responded in the affirmative to the same question in July 1981, shortly after the Israeli bombing of PLO and DFLP Headquarters in Beirut. Gallup poll for *Newsweek,* as reported in *Jerusalem Post,* September 7, 1981.

57   57% of those polled explained their position by saying they believed the Iraqis were "planning to make nuclear bombs." A Roper poll of August 1981 in Curtiss, *Changing Image,* p. 205.

58   In the wake of the 1981 Beirut bombing, Americans opposed the resumption of shipment to Israel of American-made F-16 aircraft by a majority of 61:30 (with 9% not expressing an opinion). *Jerusalem Post,* September 7, 1981. For public attitudes toward the bombing of PLO and DFLP headquarters in Beirut and F-16 delivery, see also, *International Herald Tribune,* July 28, 1981. A related manifestation of American misgivings about the Beirut bombing was a 28% poor rating for Prime Minister Begin's efforts for peace – almost triple the disapproval rate in 1978. Among American Jews, 50% believed that "Begin's policies eroded American support for Israel." *Newsweek,* September 7, 1981, reporting Gallup findings of July 1981. It is noteworthy that in early 1978, Americans justified Israel's "Litani Operation" in Lebanon by a 47:40% plurality. Louis Harris Poll, March 30, 1978.

59   See Table IX where the figures for "June 1982" and "August 1982" are from polls taken after the launching of the Israeli operation. Interestingly, the American public had been more critical of the July 1981 bombing in Beirut than during the early phases of the 1982 war. According to *Newsweek,* Gallup found 50% expressing disapproval and 31% approval of the 1981 raid. *Chicago Sun Times,* July 4, 1982.

60   On July 11, 1982, the *Los Angeles Times* reported 60% positive public ratings for Israeli Prime Minister Menachem Begin. This compared with 53% in March and 43% in January 1982. *Yediot Aharonot,* July 12, 1982.

61   The *Los Angeles Times,* July 11, 1982. See also, *National Journal,* July 24, 1982, p. 1315.

62   See Table IX above.

63   *Washington Post,* September 26, 1982.

64   See "Begin's Handling of Sharon Case Worries Americans," *The Harris Survey* (# 15, 1983), February 20, 1983. The noted Gallup poll of late September 1982 (see Table IX) also found Americans accusing Begin of undermining US support for Israel (by 70% of respondents). *Newsweek,* October 4, 1982. See also Gallup poll of March 1983 where Americans listed Begin among the world's five least popular leaders. *Ma'ariv,* March 15, 1983.

65   See Table IX above.

66   *Washington Post,* October 21, 1981.

67   David Garth polls, *Yediot Aharonot,* May 20, 1982.

68   The findings were:

	Yes	No	DK
April 1980	33%	37%	30%
July 1981	31	44	25
August 1982	37	45	18
November 1982	33	50	17

For 1980, 1981 and August 1982 see Connie De Boer, "The Polls: The Arab-Israeli Conflict," *Public Opinion Quarterly,* Spring 1983, p. 126. For November 1982 see "National Survey" (Institute of Arab Studies, Inc.), November 1982 (unpublished report), n.p.

69   A David Garth poll as reported in *Yediot Aharonot,* May 20, 1982.

70   Louis Harris polls, as reported in *Ha'aretz,* October 3, 1980.

71   Louis Harris found 52% of those questioned opposed to both propositions. *Yediot Aharonot,* October 3, 1980. A ratio of 65:10 support for the Israeli position on Jerusalem was found by the Middle East Institute (MEI) in the fall of 1980. Shelley Slade, "The Image of the Arab in America," p. 154.

72   The findings of support for Israel's position and their sources are:
     Mid-1977; 40%, Yankelovitz *et al, Los Angeles Times,* July 29, 1981;
     Late 1977; 44%, Louis Harris, The *Washington Post,* November 18, 1977;
     Late 1979; 55%, Louis Harris, *Yediot Aharonot,* October 3, 1980;
     Late 1980: 65%, Louis Harris, *B'nai B'rith Messenger* October, 17, 1980;
Moreover, in April 1982, 75% of those who claimed to know what the PLO was, believed it to be "a force for war rather than peace." ABC News/*Washington Post* poll, *Washington Post,* May 5, 1982.

73   Louis Harris, as reported in the *New York Post,* January 23, 1978.

74   Harris Survey as reported in William C. Adams, "Middle East Meets West," p. 52.

75   Harris findings, *Yediot Aharonot,* October 3, 1980. Italics added.

76   Harris poll, *Heritage,* July 23, 1982.

77   In a February 1977 Roper survey, 55% supported that position.

78   Gallup poll of January 1978. See Curtiss, *Changing Image,* pp. 193, 195.

79   *A Study of the Attitudes of the American People and the American Jewish Community Toward the Arab-Israeli Conflict in the Middle East* (Study No. 804011), Louis Harris and Associates, Inc., prepared for Edgar M. Bronfman, Chairman, The Seagram Company, Ltd., and Acting President, World Jewish Congress, September 1980. Table 42, p. 101.

80   56% supported this proposition. *Yediot Aharonot,* October 3, 1980. It should be noted, however, that there appears to be little intensity in the support for the "independent state" option. In October 1981, two-thirds of the respondents to an NBC News/AP poll said they did not know enough about the issue to have an opinion. Adams, "Middle East Meets West," p. 53.

81   By 66%. *Yediot Aharonot,* October 3, 1980.

82   57% supported that suggestion. Shelley Slade, "The Image of the Arab in America," p. 155.

83   Louis Harris, *Ha'aretz,* October 19, 1980.

84   Louis Harris survey, June 18 and 22, 1982, as reported in *Near East Report,* vol. xxv, no. 28 (July 9, 1982), p. 139. See also *Washington Post,* July 11, 1982.

85   The two *Washington Post*/ABC News polls were conducted in late August and March 1982 respectively. See *International Herald Tribune,* August 24, 1982.

86   *American Attitudes Toward the Palestine Question* (Belmont, Mass: Institute of Arab Studies, Inc.), November 1982, n.p.

87   For a similar assessment see Thomas L. Hughes, "Up from Reaganism," *Foreign Policy,* no. 44 (Fall 1981), p. 9.

88   Thus, for example, while over 40% of those questioned in June and again in early and mid-July 1982 supported such American involvement in order to

facilitate a settlement in Lebanon, the majority was opposed. See Harris survey as reported in the *Washington Post*, July 11, 19, 1982.

89   For specific examples see Chapter 2, below.

90   In April 1978, 65% of the public (and 73% of college graduates) felt that Sadat was speaking for Egypt only and that other Arab states did not share his pursuit of peace with Israel. CBS poll, as reported in Richard H. Curtiss, *Changing Image*, p. 197.

91   Yet, even the Egyptian precedent (or exception) is not unambiguous. The fact that 68% of those surveyed in an October 1981 NBC News/AP poll agreed that President Sadat's death would "hurt the chances for peace in the Middle East" suggests that the personal popularity of the late Egyptian leader had played a major role in shaping American public attitudes toward Egypt. Indeed, in 1980 a Harris study found that Americans viewed Sadat as the most respected and most trusted leader in the Middle East, and that he was "more respected than most public figures in the United States." See Adams, "Middle East Meets West," p. 51.

92   As noted in fn. 56, above, in July 1980 a Harris poll asked Americans for their opinion on the question of withholding economic and military aid from Israel in order to facilitate a more compromising position within the peace process. 44% approved an American *threat* to withhold aid. 37% opposed even the threat. 50% opposed any sanctions if these could lead to an Arab military edge vis-à-vis Israel. 25% were willing to support such measures regardless of the consequences for Israel's security. Curtiss, *Changing Image*, p. 205.

Chapter 2

1   See, for example, Thomas M. Frank and Edward Weisband, *Foreign Policy by Congress* (New York: Oxford University Press, 1979); Edward A. Kolodzeij, "Formulating Foreign Policy," in Richard M. Pious (ed.), *The Power to Govern* (Vermont: The Academy of Political Science, 1981), pp. 174-189; and Feuerwerger, *Congress and Israel*.

2   See Kolodzeij, "Formulating Foreign Policy," pp. 187-189. See also David M. Abshire, "Foreign Policy Makers: President vs. Congress," in David M. Abshire and Ralph D. Nurenberger (eds.), *The Growing Power of Congress* (California: Sage, 1981), pp. 22-114, particularly pp. 92ff.

3   See, for example, the discussion on "The Impact of Congress on National Security Policy," in Amos A. Jordan and William J. Taylor, Jr., *American National Security: Policy and Process* (Maryland: John Hopkins University Press, 1981), pp. 109-126.

4   See discussion in Introduction above.

5   Donald R. Mathews and James A. Stimson, "Decision-making by U.S. Representatives: A Preliminary Model," in S. Sidney Ulmer (ed.), *Political Decision-Making* (New York: Van Nostrand Reinhold, 1970), pp. 14-43. See also their *Yeas and Nays: Normal Decision-Making in the U.S. House of Representatives* (New York: Wiley, 1975).

6   David Graham, "Factors Shaping Congressional Support for Israel During the 93rd Congress," *The Jerusalem Journal of International Relations*, vol. 2, no. 3 (Spring 1978), pp. 23-45.

7   William B. Quandt, "Domestic Influences," pp. 280-81.

8   See "Public Attitudes: The Middle East," Chapter 1, above.

9   Marvin C. Feuerwerger, *Congress and Israel,* pp. 11, 28.

10 See "Can Foreign Aid Be Spared?" Chapter 5, below.

11 For example, for the period 1970-1977 Congress increased total aid to Israel by 8.7%. This included a 30% increase in economic aid and a 3% increase in military aid. Feuerwerger, *Congress and Israel,* pp. 29-30. On more recent congressional involvement, see "Can Foreign Aid Be Spared," below.

12 See, for example, Public Law (PL) 94-329 (1976), in which Congress mandated that military aid to Israel for FY 1976-77 be repaid in *no less* than twenty years, following a grace period of ten years on repayments of the principal. Moreover, the authorization waived one-half of the repayment.

13 In FY 1979 Congress appropriated an unrequested $20 million for the construction of a nuclear power and desalinating plant in Israel. In FY 1972 it initiated a security assistance program in Israel. For the latter, see *National Journal,* January 8, 1972, pp. 57-72.

14 Although it was rarely asked to appropriate funds specifically for Israel, Congress, on its own initiative has earmarked virtually all funds for Israel since the early 1970s. Clyde R. Mark, *Foreign Assistance to the State of Israel: A Compilation of Basic Data,* Congressional Research Service Report No. 76-185 (Washington, D.C., Library of Congress, 1976), p. 3.

15 In 1974, for example, Congress appropriated $133 million to relieve Israel of debts incurred as a result of the American resupply operation during the Yom Kippur War. *Congressional Quarterly Almanac,* 1974, p. 591.

16 In 1976 Congress ignored the threat of a presidential veto and appropriated $275 million for the "transition quarter" created between FY 1976 and 1977 by the change in dates of the American fiscal year. See, *Congressional Quarterly Almanac* (1976), pp. 754-55.

17 William B. Quandt, "Domestic Influences," p. 274.

18 William B. Quandt, *Decade of Decisions* (Berkeley: University of California Press, 1977), p. 270.

19 Section 36 (b) of the 1976 Arms Export Control Act (PL 94-329).

20 *Congressional Quarterly Almanac,* 1973, p. 820.

21 *Ibid.,* 1974, p. 546.

22 *Ibid.,* 1975, p. 358.

23 *Ibid.,* 1976, p. 253.

24 *Ibid.,* 1977, p. 387.

25 See this author's *Weapons to Riyadh: US Policy and Regional Security* (Tel Aviv: CSS Memorandum, No. 4, April 1981), p. 8. See also, *Congressional Quarterly Almanac,* 1978, p. 405.

26 *Ibid.* See also discussion in Chapter 6, below.

27 Feuerwerger, *Congress and Israel,* pp. 176-190.

28 See discussion of the FY 1983 foreign aid bill in Chapter 4, below.

29 See *Congressional Quarterly,* May 15, 1982, p. 1161; August 22, 1981, p. 1524, respectively.

30 See discussion in the Introduction above.

31 *Congress and Foreign Policy - 1975,* Committee on International Relations, House of Representatives (Washington, DC: USPGO), 1976, p. 158.

32 *Disapprove Construction Projects on the Island of Diego Garcia,* Hearings,

Senate Armed Services Committee on Senate Resolution 160, June 10, 1975, pp. 47; 43 respectively.

33   This statement was later labeled "The Carter Doctrine." For the complete State of the Union address, see *Weekly Compilation of Presidential Documents*, January 23, 1980, p. 197.

34   For broad-based congressional support see, for example, *Washington Post* and *New York Times*, January 24, 1980.

35   *Weekly Compilation.*

36   See discussion of Selective Interventionism in Chapter 1 above.

37   For public attitudes toward the use of American troops, see "The 'Turn to the Right' and Foreign/Security Policies," as well as the conclusions, Chapter 1, above.

38   For a discussion of President Reagan's "extended honeymoon," see introduction to this author's *Encounter with Reality: Reagan and the Middle East During the First Term* (Westview Press and Jerusalem Post for JCSS: 1985).

39   *Congressional Quarterly*, January 9, 1982, p. 61; January 15, 1983, p. 107.

40   *National Journal*, May 8, 1982, p. 807.

41   *Congressional Quarterly*, January 9, 1982, p. 50.

42   *Ibid.*

43   See, for example, the case of Foreign Relations Committee Chairman Charles Percy, *Congressional Quarterly*, March 14, 1981, pp. 477-78.

44   *Congressional Quarterly*, January 9, 1982, p. 50.

45   *National Journal*, May 8, 1982, p. 810.

46   *National Review*, December 10, 1982, p. 1520. Concurrently, one quarter of liberal Republicans did not return to the 98th Congress. *Ibid.*

47   According to David R. Gergen, White House Director of Communications, during the 97th Congress the administration had a "pool of 77 Democrats willing to support the policies when the need arose. Three of them did not win re-election in 1982." Yet he saw the potential for another 12 in the 98th Congress. *Congressional Quarterly*, November 13, 1982, p. 2837.

48   In 1982 in the House of Representatives, southern Democrats voted with southern Republicans 66% of the time. In the Senate, southern Democrats voted with southern Republicans 73% of the time. *Congressional Quarterly*, January 15, 1983, p. 101. See also detailed tables of voting patterns in *National Journal*, May 8, 1982, pp. 801-810. See also the findings of *Opinion Outlook*, whereby 84 of the 125 southern congressional districts were found to be among America's 87 most conservative districts. In *National Journal*, November 14, 1981, p. 2033.

49   *National Journal*, May 8, 1982, pp. 801-810.

50   See William Schneider's study in *Opinion Outlook*, November 2, 1982.

51   These involve areas where newcomers constitute a majority or at least a sizable minority within a relatively short time of their arrival in their new area of residence. Florida is an obvious example.

52   Schneider in *Opinion Outlook*. See also the analysis of Richard M. Scammon, "The Impact of Population Shifts," in Richard M. Pious, *The Power to Govern* (New York: The Academy of Political Science, 1981), pp. 214-221.

53   *National Journal*, November 14, 1981, pp. 2019, 2036. See also, Scammon, "The Impact of Population Shifts." These predictions began to materialize in 1980-81, as the South and West continued to gain population at the expense of the Northeast and Midwest regions. Interestingly, the South's gain in 1980-81 was more than double that of 1975-76. "Geographic Mobility: March 1980-March 1981" (Washing-

ton, DC: US Bureau of Census, 1983), as quoted in *National Journal,* February 19, 1983, p. 398. See also, "A Statistical Portrait of a Changing America," *National Journal,* October 29, 1983, p. 2201.

54 *Ibid.*

55 On the correlation between conservatism and Selective Interventionism, see Chapter 1, above. Interestingly, in this context, the major distinction between the more extremely conservative, semi-isolationists on the one hand, and the more moderate "selective-interventionists" on the other, is the greater emphasis of the former on the exclusive use of naval forces rather than any ground involvement in remote areas of the globe.

56 *US News & World Report,* February 28, 1983.

57 *Ibid.*

58 *Congressional Quarterly,* January 3, 1981, pp. 3-4. On the relevancy of support from big business, see "Petrodollars and Foreign/Security Policies: The Role of 'Big Business,'" Chapter 6, below.

59 Noteworthy is the fact that during the past two decades Jewish representation has more than tripled from 2% in 1961 to 7.1% in 1982. Thus, according to the Census Bureau estimates, Jews today enjoy a voice in Congress that far exceeds their 2.3% share of the population-at-large. See discussion in Chapter 3, below.

60 *New York Times*/CBS poll, *Near East Report,* November 12, 1982.

61 *Davar* (Hebrew), July 24, 1983.

62 See Novik, *Encounter With Reality.*

63 See Chapter 4, below.

64 Blunt criticism of Israel's West Bank settlement policy that accompanied Congressional approval of increased FY 1983 aid to Israel was a manifestation of this new phenomenon. See Chapter 4, below.

65 For the most thorough statement of this concept see George E. Ball, "How to Save Israel In Spite of Herself," *Foreign Affairs,* vol. 55, no. 3 (April 1977), pp. 453-471.

Chapter 3

1 Charles Mathias, "Ethnic Groups and Foreign Policy," *Foreign Affairs,* vol. 59, no. 5 (Summer 1981), p. 993. In 1981 a Yankelovich, Skelly and White poll, commissioned by the American Jewish Committee, found 48% of respondents in agreement with the statement that "Jews are more loyal to Israel than to America." Just under 25% accepted the statement that "Jews have too much power in the U.S." Quoted in Nathan Perlmutter and Ruth Perlmutter, *The Real Antisemitism* (NY: Arbor House, 1982), p. 76.

2 As quoted in Milton Himmelfarb and David Singer (eds.), *American Jewish Year Book (AJYB) 1983* (NY: The American Jewish Committee; Philadelphia: The Jewish Publication Society of America, 1983), p. 65.

3 See, for example, the statement attributed to *Public Opinion* co-editor Ben Watenberg, that "God gave the Arabs a lot of oil, and gave the Jews a lot of clout in the Electoral College." *International Herald Tribune,* October 25, 1980.

4 With the possible exception of the Jewish aggregation under the Czarist regime

in Russia on the eve of the mass migration. Daniel Elazar, "The Geography of American Jewish Communal Life," *Congressional Bi-Weekly,* vol 40, no. 2 (January 26, 1973), p. 10.

5   Even this figure is subject to debate. See discussion below.

6   The literature on Jewish demography demonstrates sensitivity to these problems. See, for example, the annual studies of American Jewish demography in the 1980-1983 volumes of the *AJYB.*

7   "Religion Reported by the Civilian Population of the U.S., March 1957," *Current Population Reports* (Washington, DC: US Bureau of the Census, 1958), Series P-20, no. 79.

8   *AJYB 1981,* p. 4.

9   Steven M. Cohen, "The 1981-1982 National Survey of American Jews," *AJYB 1983,* pp. 89-110; Steven M. Cohen, "The 1983 National Survey of American Jews and Jewish Communal Leaders" (New York: Institute on American-Jewish Relations, The American Jewish Committee), September 1983. The 1983 survey of community leaders was restricted to five of the major Jewish organizations. Steven M. Cohen, "Case of Distortion or Disappointment?" *Jerusalem Post,* February 9, 1984.

10   Steven M. Cohen, "The 1981-1982 National Survey," p. 90.

11   "Net" Jewish population refers to the total population excluding non-Jewish members of Jewish households.

12   See, for example, Saul B. Cohen, "Israel-US-American Jewry: Changing Relations," *Congress Monthly,* September-October 1980, p. 13.

13   *AJYB 1983,* p. 128; *AJYB 1981,* pp. 32, 170. See also Jack Diamond, "How many Jews in New York City?" *Congress Monthly,* vol. 45, no. 1 (January 1978), p. 8.

14   *AJYB 1983,* p. 143. Characteristically, this figure is smaller by over 300,000 than the total sum of reported constituencies of local Jewish federations. *AJYB 1981,* p. 170.

15   *AJYB 1981,* pp. 8, 56.

16   Based on calculation of figures presented in Appendix to Alvin Chenkin and Maynard Miran, "Jewish Population in the United States, 1979," *AJYB 1980,* pp. 161-171.

17   See also Alan M. Fishner, "Realignment of the Jewish Vote?" *Political Science Quarterly,* vol. 94, no. 1 (Spring 1979), p. 97, as well as Steven Bauman, "Electoral Reform and American Jewry," *Congress Monthly,* vol. 45, no. 1 (January 1978), p. 6.

18   *Congressional Quarterly,* November 8, 1980, p. 3297. In 1976 the turnout was 54.4%. *Ibid.*

19   The American Jewish Committee, *The 1981 National Survey of American Jews* (NSAJ) (unpublished monograph, n.p., n.d.), p. 1.

20   For a detailed annotated list of American Jewish organizations, see *AJYB 1983,* pp. 283-325.

21   For an analysis of Jewish income levels see Alvin Chenkin, "The National Gallup Polls and American Jewish Demography," *AJYB 1983,* p. 125.

22   David Silverberg, "Power, Politics and Change," *Present Tense,* vol. 8, no. 2 (Winter 1981), pp. 24-25.

23   *National Journal,* May 7, 1983, p. 935.

24   John J. Fialka, "Pro Israel Politics," *Wall Street Journal,* August 3, 1983, pp. 1, 15.

25   In 1982 Jewish PACs spent over $355,000 in races affecting the composition of

the Foreign Affairs Committee and the Foreign Operations Subcommittee of the Appropriations Committee of the House; over $230,000 in support of six members of the Senate Appropriations Committee; and over $78,000 in helping elect a Democratic senator from Maine. *Ibid.*

26 *Ibid.* Similarly, 28 PACs, all based outside of Maine, contributed to the successful senatorial campaign of George Mitchelle in that state. *Ibid.*

27 Melvin Swig, Chairman of Bay Area Citizens PAC, as quoted in *Ibid.*

28 As quoted in David Silverberg, "Power, Politics and Change," p. 22.

29 By 1980 the percentage of American-born among American Jewry was well above 70%. Moreover, one out of every five was already third generation native American. *AJYB 1981,* pp. 42, 43. In 1981 the American Jewish Committee-sponsored *NSAJ* found 90% of respondents identifying themselves as American born; 46% were second generation native Americans. *NSAJ,* P. 5.

30 See also Morris Amitay's article in *Jewish Community Bulletin,* July 4, 1983.

31 Alan M. Fisher's study as quoted in Dick Kirschten, "Reagan Looks to Religious Leaders for Continuing Support in 1984," *National Journal,* August 20, 1983, pp. 1727, 1730.

32 The actual 1981/2 return was 35% "strongly agree;" 41% "agree;" 17% "disagree;" 3% "strongly disagree;" 4% "not sure." The 1983 data from Steven M. Cohen (1983), "The 1983 National Survey," p. 13.

33 Jonathan Kirsh, "Sentimental Politics," *New West,* January 28, 1980, p. 16.

34 For early signs of changes that may undermine some of these multipliers of political influence, see discussion below.

35 See discussion, Chapter 1 above.

36 See footnote 29 above.

37 In a 1981 survey 75% of the community were found to be supportive of "stronger measures against illegal immigrants." *NSAJ,* see Table XIV.

38 Both single-community studies of Jewish demography (e.g., Boston, 1965-1975) and general surveys have pointed out the growing share of white collar among Jewish workers. By 1970, for example, compared with less than 40% of the general population, some 87% of Jewish males and 89% of Jewish females occupied white collar positions. *AJYB 1981,* p. 52. See also Nathan Glazer, "The American Jew and the Attainment of a Middle-Class Rank: Some Trends and Explanations," in Marshall Sklare (ed.), *The Jews* (Glencoe 1958), p. 138. Equally telling are the findings about Jewish representation among the better educated. By 1970 51.6% of Jews were found to have had some college education compared with 22.4% among non-Jewish Whites. *AJYB 1981,* p. 49.

39 In 1982 over one-third of Jews surveyed identified themselves as liberals; 17% as conservatives. *AJYB 1983,* p. 102. In 1983 the division was 36:23. Steven M. Cohen, "The 1983 National Survey," p. 31.

40 On both issues, see, for example, Irving Louis Horowitz, "Jews and the 1980 Elections," *Jewish Spectator,* Fall 1980, p. 17; Alan M. Fisher, "Realignment of the Jewish Vote?" *Political Science Quarterly,* vol. 94, no. 1 (Spring 1979), p. 100; Nathan Perlmuter "Domestic Realignments and a Changing Jewish Community: Implications for U.S. Policy," in Nimrod Novik (ed.), *Israel in US Foreign and Security Policy* (Tel Aviv, JCSS), 1983, pp. 5-16.

41 *AJYB 1982,* p. 92.

42 *Ibid.*

43 See Earl Raab, "American Jewish Attitudes on Israel: Consensus and Dissent,"

Perspectives, November 1981, p. 9; Fisher, "Realignment of the Jewish Vote?" AJYB 1982, pp. 92, 94-95; Perlmutter, "Domestic Realignments."

44 AJYB 1982, pp. 94-95.

45 For American Jewish Attitudes toward specific Israeli policies see discussion below.

46 See discussion, Chapter 1 above.

47 On the negative correlation between liberalism and support for Israel see also AJYB 1983, pp. 108-109 as well as Seymour Martin Lipset and William Schneider, American Opinion Towards Israel and Jews (unpublished monograph), p. 41.

48 Robert J. Marx, "Saying 'No' to Jewish PACmen," Reform Judaism, Winter 1983 as quoted in International Center for Peace in the Middle East, Jews Speak Out, no. 2 (July 1983), p. 1.

49 Steve Zipperstein, "American Jewry in the 1980s," Present Tense, vol. 8, no. 2 (Winter 1981), p. 5.

50 A Yankelovitz poll of early 1982 and a Newsweek poll of September 1982 both found American Jews overwhelmingly in agreement with suggestions that anti-Semitism may be increasing as a result of anti-Israel sentiment in the US. Davar, April 3, 1983, p. 5. Newsweek, October 4, 1982, p. 11.

51 See, for example, the large collection of such statements in Jews Speak Out: Views from the Diaspora, no. 2 (July 1983), pp. 1-22.

52 NSAJ 1981, p. 3.

53 Findings of a general market survey conducted jointly by the Israel Ministry of Tourism and El Al Israel Airlines, published in Jewish Tourism to Israel, unpublished monograph (n.p., n.d.), p. 3.

54 Wall Street Journal, April 1, 1983; Milton Goldin, "Letter to the Editor," Wall Street Journal, April 13, 1982. Data on US consumer price index from US Department of Commerce, Bureau of the Census, Statistical Abstract of the United States, 1982-83 (Washington, DC: US Government Printing Office), 1982, p. 453.

55 Wall Street Journal, April 1, 1983. The UJA alone transferred to Israel a total of $2,857.7 million over the period 1969-1982. The 1982 portion of this total sum was just under three hundred million dollars. Report to the Trustees of the United Israel Appeal, Annual Report 1982 (New York: UIA), 1982, p. 16.

56 See "Signs of Change," below.

57 Los Angeles Times, November 29, 1979.

58 Jewish Post and Opinion, September 12, 1980. This July-August 1980 poll covered the greater New York area alone.

59 NSAJ 1981, p. 2. Interestingly, by late 1983 86% identified themselves that way. Steven M. Cohen, "The 1983 National Survey," p. 14.

60 Gallup poll, Newsweek, September 14, 1981.

61 Steven M. Cohen's poll, Jerusalem Post, September 14, 1982.

62 NSAJ 1981.

63 Ibid., p. 3. The findings were: 1% "strongly agree;" 11% "agree;" 17% "not sure;" 44% "disagree;" 27% "strongly disagree."

64 On the problem of data availability see "Images vs. Reality," above. The difficulties concerning data on political stands resemble the ones encountered in the search for reliable data on Jewish demography. Consequently, in this section, along with quantifiable and reliable data, the author is guilty of the error he associates with others: he resorts to less reliable and generalizable sources such as personal interviews with American Jewish leaders and intensive interaction with

an unrepresentative sample of American Jewry during the period 1970-1984.

65   See Chapter I above.

66   Senator Rudy Boschwitz (R: Minnesota), Chairman of the Senate Foreign Relations Committee's Subcommittee on the Middle East, in an interview with Wolf Blitzer, Washington correspondent of *Yediot Aharonot*, as published on December 12, 1982. Elsewhere, using the English language equivalent, he was also quoted as having said: "our economic and military assistance to Israel is a first-class bargain." In Harold P. Smith, "Our Aid to Israel is a Super Bargain," *Chicago Sun-Times*, July 22, 1983.

67   Steven J. Rosen (ed.), *The AIPAC Papers on US-Israel Relations*. See specifically Paper no. 1, *The Strategic Value of Israel;* no. 2, *Israel and the US Air Force;* no. 4, *Israel and the US Navy;* no. 5, *Israel Medical Support for the US Armed Forces;* and no. 8, *US Procurement of Israeli Defense Goods and Services* (Washington, DC: AIPAC), 1982, 1983, 1983, 1983 and 1984 respectively.

68   See, for example, article by Representative Tom Harkin (D: Iowa) entitled "Israel is our Ally," published in *The Des Moines Register* and quoted in *Near East Report*, January 14, 1983.

69   *NSAJ 1981*, p. 3.

70   For data see sources quoted in fn. 59, 60 above.

71   Gallup poll, *Newsweek*, September 14, 1981, p. 12.

72   *Newsweek*, October 4, 1982, p. 11.

73   In 1981 the *NSAJ* found 23% to hold that view. Earlier, when asked to assign blame for lack of progress in the Egyptian-Israeli negotiations, more New York Jews blamed Israel than Egypt, and more of them felt Israel's stance in the negotiations was "too difficult" than "too soft" or "about right." *Jewish Post and Opinion*, September 12, 1980.

74   The freeze had been imposed earlier, in the wake of the Israeli raid on Iraq's nuclear reactor. With the bombing of Beirut it was expanded and extended.

75   *Boston Globe*, September 17, 1982; *Los Angeles Times*, September 21, 1982; *Washington Post*, September 27, 1982.

76   Earl Raab, "American Jewish Attitudes on Israel: Consensus and Dissent," *Perspectives*, November 1981, p. 15.

77   One poll found only 10% of New York Jews in support of the return of East Jerusalem to Arab sovereignty even if Jewish access to the holy shrines were assured. *Jewish Post and Opinion*, September 12, 1980.

78   By an almost 3:1 majority they favored a freeze on settlements in order to encourage King Hussein to join the peace process. *Ha'aretz*, April 10, 1983.

79   In 1980 greater New York Jewry was found almost equally divided on the question of the desirability of a freeze. *Jewish Post and Opinion*, September 12, 1980. A more comprehensive poll of the same year found the entire community equally divided when asked whether Israel's settlement policy was an obstacle on the road to peace. *Yediot Aharonot*, November 5, 1980. In 1983 51% supported a freeze; 28% opposed and 21% were not certain. Steven M. Cohen, "The 1983 National Survey," p. 18.

80   Raab, "American Jewish Attitudes," pp. 15-16.

81   Confirming this trend, the Gallup organization concluded that "changes in the Jewish population closely parallel national changes although they are of greater magnitude." Alan M. Fisher, "The National Gallup Polls and American Jewish Demography," *AJYB 1983*, p. 121. See also *AJYB 1981*, p. 57.

82　It has been suggested that, on the average, new migrants tend to become active in their new community only five years after establishing new residency. Moreover, in most instances they do not reach the level of intensity of the involvement of a native. Basil Zimmer, "Participatory Migrants in Urban Structures," *American Sociological Review*, 1955, pp. 218-224.

83　*AJYB 1980*, pp. 32-33.

84　*Ibid.*, p. 50.

85　See, for example, *Wall Steet Journal*, April 13, 1983; Rabbi Arthur Herzberg "Yahadut Artsot Habrit: Beayot Kiumiot" (US Jewry: Existential Problems), *Ha'aretz*, March 28, 1983.

86　Saul B. Cohen, "Israel-US-American Jewry: Changing Relations," p. 13.

87　Hertzberg, "Yahadut Artsot Habrit."

88　In late 1981 53% of American Jews were found supportive of the suggestion that "Begin's policies [were] hurting support for Israel in the U.S." Gallup poll, *Newsweek*, September 14, 1981, p. 12. In the aftermath of the Sabra and Shatila massacres, 78% felt that way. *Newsweek*, October 4, 1982. In late 1983, as emotions charged by the dramatic events of the summer and fall of 1982 were again calm, 50% of the community continued to share that sentiment. Steven M. Cohen, "The 1983 National Survey," p. 23.

89　The *NSAJ 1981* found 57% supportive of the right to dissent. A 1982 Gallup poll found 31% advocating an "active role in affecting Israel's policies" for American Jewry. *Newsweek*, October 4, 1982. In 1980 an estimated 70% of New York Jewry were in agreement with the right to publicly criticize Israeli policies. *Jewish Post and Opinion*, September 12, 1980.

90　As quoted in *The Washington Post*, September 2, 1982; *New York Times*, September 8, 1982.

91　On the popularity of the formula as a desirable principle for Arab-Israeli settlement see Chapter 1, above.

Chapter 4

1　*Congressional Quarterly*, November 8, 1980, p. 3350.

2　US tax laws prevent organizations that wish to maintain their non-profit (tax-exempt) status from engaging in active political campaigning.

3　*Congressional Quarterly*, September 6, 1980, p. 2627.

4　These include Howard J. Phillips and the Conservative Caucus; Ed McAteer and the Religious Round Table; Phyllis Schlafly and the Eagle Forum; Terry Dolan and the NCPAC; M. Stanton Evans, a *Human Events* columnist; James V. Lacy of Young Americans for Freedom; William A. Rusher, publisher of *National Review;* Paul M. Weyrich and his Committee for the Survival of a Free Congress; Mickey Edwards and the American Conservative Union, among others. William F. Buckley, Jr., editor of *National Review*, is considered by many as their intellectual "guru."

5　Cal Thomas, Moral Majority's Vice President for Communications, *National Journal*, May 2, 1981, p. 780.

6　John D. Lofton, Jr., editor of *Conservative Digest*, as quoted in *Ibid.*

7　NCPAC said it had spent $4.5 million in the 1980 campaign, including $1.2 million in campaign expenditures against liberal Senate incumbents. *Congressional Quarterly*, November 15, 1980, p. 3372. For a convincing analysis suggesting a much more limited impact of New Right efforts in the 1980 elections, see Seymour Martin Lipset, "Failures of Extremism," *Society*, November/December 1982, p. 56.

8 Cal Thomas, *National Journal*, May 2, 1981, p. 781.

9 Arthur J. Finkelstein, *Congressional Quarterly* November 15, 1981, p. 3373. Former Senator George McGovern found his "favorability rating" dropped 20% during NCPAC's pre-primary anti-McGovern advertising campaign. *Ibid.*

10 Findings of campaign surveys in Alabama and Oklahoma. *Ibid.*

11 Ruth W. Mouly, "Israel: Darling of the Religious Right," *The Humanist*, May/June 1982, p. 10.

12 *New York Times*, July 4, 1982.

13 *New York Times*, August 1, 1982.

14 As quoted in the *Los Angeles Herald Examiner*, November 13, 1982.

15 In a mailgram to president-elect Reagan, signed jointly by Rev. Jerry Falwell, Edward E. McAteer and Paul Weyrich. Quoted in Nathan Perlmutter and Ruth Ann Perlmutter, *The Real Anti-Semitism*, p. 167.

16 *Moral Majority Report*, March 16, 1981, p. 22.

17 *Ibid.*, p. 4.

18 Steven L. Spiegel, "Religious Components of U.S. Middle East Policy," *Journal of International Affairs*, Fall/Winter 1982/3, pp. 238-239.

19 One manifestation of the counteroffensive has been the dramatic growth in liberal Political Action Committees (PACs). Of the six PACs supporting liberal candidates in 1982, five did not exist in 1980. In 1981 they raised some $4 million. This was less than a third of the funds raised by their conservative counterparts, but almost four times the comparable liberal figure for 1979. *Congressional Quarterly*, February 27, 1982, p. 482.

20 Bill Keller, "Evangelical Conservatives Move from Pews to Polls, But Can They Sway Congress?" *Congressional Quarterly*, September 6, 1980, p. 2632.

21 *Washington Post*, September 12, 1981. This view draws on the Christian right's favorite passage from the Scriptures in Genesis 12:3 referring to God's promise to Israel: "I will bless them that bless you and curse them that curse you."

22 In an interview in *Christianity Today* as quoted in Ruth W. Mouly, "Israel: Darling of the Religious Right," p. 5.

23 Geoffrey Wigoder, "Stressing the Fundamentals," *Jerusalem Post Magazine*, April 16, 1982, p. 4.

24 *Washington Post*, March 23,; October 30, 1981.

25 Franklin H. Littel, "Christian Congress for Israel," *Near East Report*, November 20, 1982, p. 213.

26 *Jerusalem Post*, February 24, 1982.

27 *Ha'aretz*, December 6, 1981; *Jerusalem Post*, February 24, 1982.

28 *New York Times*, February 24, 1982.

29 According to one investigation the number of communications with members of Congress on behalf of the anti-AWACS lobby that originated with identifiable Religious Right members was "infinitesimal." Ruth W. Mouly, "Israel: Darling of the Religious Right," p. 11.

30 At the end of his first year in office the New Right awarded President Reagan a grade of "C to C-minus." Among a torrent of complaints, presidential appointments in particular were reported to have caused them considerable "grief." *The Economist*, June 5, 1982.

31 The 1982 mid-term elections were a clear testimony to the organization's

failure: it was unable to unseat any of those targeted for its negative campaign save one. See also Spiegel, "Religious Components," p. 243.

32 *Congressional Quarterly*, September 6, 1980, p. 2632. See also Seymour Martin Lipset and Earl Raab, "The Election and the Evangelicals," *Commentary*, March 1981, p. 25; Seymour Martin Lipset, "Failure of Extremism," p. 54.

33 *Congressional Quarterly*, September 6, 1980, p. 2632.

34 *Washington Post*, ABC News poll, as reported in the *Washington Post*, June 13, 1981.

35 *Ibid.*

36 Poll by Richard Wirthlin, *Time*, November 15, 1982, p. 18.

37 Lipset and Raab, "The Election and the Evangelicals," p. 26. See also Earl Raab, "Fundamentalists: Real and Phantom Concerns," *ADL Bulletin*, January 1982, pp. 12-14.

38 Ruth W. Mouly, "Israel: Darling of the Religious Right."

39 See, for example, *Time*, June 1, 1981.

40 While most Americans retained their traditional labels − "conservative," "moderate" or "liberal" − the content of those identities has shifted to the right (as defined in Chapter One, above).

41 Lipset and Raab, "The Election and the Evangelists," p. 30.

42 One example of the media's contribution to the image of political potency was the coverage given by more than 250 press and broadcast representatives to the movement's August 1980 revival meeting in Dallas. *Congressional Quarterly*, September 6, 1980, p. 2627.

43 For brief reviews of the Jewish dilemma with the Moral Majority see, for example, *AJYB 1982*, pp. 101-104; Rabbi Ronald B. Sobel, "The Christian Right," unpublished monograph of a lecture delivered at the Anti-Defamation League of B'nei B'rith NEC Meeting, Dallas, Texas, October 25, 1980; Jack R. Fischel, "The Fundamentalist Perception of Jews," *Midstream*, December 1982, pp. 30-31. In listing the three most pressing problems between the American and Israeli Jewish communities, Stuart Eisenstadt included the attitude of Israeli Prime Minister Menachem Begin toward the Moral Majority's Rev. Falwell. *Davar*, April 3, 1983.

44 Rabbi Arthur Hertzberg, as quoted in *Congressional Quarterly*, August 22, 1981, p. 1526.

45 *Ibid.* For a more forceful presentation of this view, see statement by Earl Raab, executive director of the Jewish Community Relations Council of San Francisco, as released by ADL press office, October 21, 1981. See also Nathan Perlmutter, National Director, ADL, "Rethinking Friendships," *ADL Bulletin*, December 1982, p. 2.

46 On November 20, 1983 Begin, in a rare exception to his post-resignation rule of seclusion, held a brief conversation with Falwell. A few days earlier, Defense Minister Arens had told a Falwell-led Moral Majority delegation that the US should accept permanent Israeli control over the West Bank.

Chapter 5

1 Senator Jesse Helms (R: North Carolina), quoted in *Congressional Quarterly*, April 17, 1982, p. 860. According to official Department of State figures, by 1982 the total figure was $220 billion. *US News & World Report*, December 13, 1982, p. 57.

2   Representative C.W. Bill Young (R: Florida), *US News & World Report*, March 31, 1980, p. 59.

3   Representative Robert E. Bauman (R: Maryland), in *Ibid.*

4   U.S. Department of State data as quoted in *US News & World Report*, December 13, 1982, p. 58.

5   See discussion in *Congressional Quarterly Almanac: 96th Congress, 2nd Session – 1980*, p. 198.

6   *Congressional Quarterly Almanac*, 1980, p. 313.

7   ABC News/*Washington Post* poll of October 1981, as reported by Adams, "Middle East Meets West," p. 55.

8   NBC News poll, released on March 31, 1978. See also Table VII above.

9   John Felton, "Budget Cutting Fervor, Politics, Add New Burdens for Foreign Aid Programs," Congressional Quarterly, October 25, 1980, p. 3214.

10   David M. Abshire, "Foreign Policy Makers: President vs. Congress," in Abshire and Ralph M. Nurnberger (eds.), *The Growing Power of Congress* (California: Sage Publications, 1981), p. 79.

11   See, for example, *Congressional Quarterly*, July 3, 1982, pp. 1578-79. Commenting on the FY 1983 aid bill, one supporter was quoted as having suggested that the decision of the House Foreign Affairs Committee to increase aid to Israel was meant to help get the bill passed. *Congressional Quarterly*, May 22, 1982, p. 1179. In the words of Rep. Charles Wilson (D: Texas), "if it wasn't for Israel, we couldn't pass a foreign aid bill." "The American-Israeli connection," *CBS Report*, CBS Television Network, June 17, 1982 (p. 10 of transcript).

12   Signs of disappointment with Israel's ability to put her own economic house in order were observable as of early 1984. Administration officials and legislators alike demanded of Israel to do more in helping herself while asking Washington to increase its contribution. See, for example, *Davar*, March 4, 1984; *Newsweek*, August 27, 1984, p. 5.

13   See Chapter 6, below.

14   "The American-Israeli Connection," *CBS Report*.

15   See Chapter 1, above.

16   The actual figure was $764 million as the US "loaned" $21 million for emergency assistance to El Salvador and Liberia. The FY 1982 $806 million includes "repayment" of that loan. See Table XXII.

17   Note also the criticism of Israel's bombing of Iraq's Osirak nuclear facility and Jerusalem's active opposition to the Saudi "AWACS deal."

18   The discussion in the following pages draws primarily on the following articles by Richard Whittle: "Big Increase Asked for Foreign Military Aid," *Congressional Quarterly*, February 13, 1982, 253-256; "Key House Panel Rejects Aid Plan...But Boosts Aid to Israel and Turkey," *Congressional Quarterly*, May 1, 1982, 1012-1013; "House Panel Adopts Half of Arms Aid Boost," *Congressional Quarterly*, May 22, 1982, 1179-1185; "Senate Panel Would Freeze Foreign Aid for El Salvador," *Congressional Quarterly*, May 29, 1982, 1255-1257 as well as (no author) "Budget Resolution Forces Aid Choices... With Supporters of Israel First in Line," *Congressional Quarterly*, July 3, 1982, pp. 1578-9; G. Neal Lendenmann, "The Struggle in Congress over Aid Levels to Israel," *American-Arab Affairs*, no. 3 (Winter 1982-83), pp. 83-93.

19   This sentiment was expressed, for example, by several congressmen in response to the administration's requests in February 1982. *Congressional*

Quarterly, February 13, 1982, p. 253.

20   An administration cannot undertake to guarantee a loan without congressional authorization. Yet, congressional appropriation of funds is obviously not required. For the significance of this distinction, see discussion below.

21   Francis West, Assistant Secretary of Defense for International Security Assistance, in testimony to the Senate Foreign Relations Committee. *Jerusalem Post*, April 16, 1982.

22   The actual figure for FY 1982 was $806 million, yet it included $21 million that Congress added to replace shortfalls from FY 1981.

23   The only exception was in FY 1979. Yet, the allocation then included special aid promised by President Carter in the context of the negotiations for the Israeli-Egyptian peace treaty. This included $800 million earmarked for the construction of two air bases to substitute for the ones abandoned in the Sinai. *Congressional Quarterly Almanac 1979*, pp. 137-141.

24   Quoted in *US News and World Report*, December 13, 1982, p. 58.

25   According to most accounts, it was assumed by May that Congress was going to adopt that course. Interviews in Washington, DC, February 1983. See also Lendenmann, "The Struggle in Congress," pp. 87-88.

26   See Yankelovich, *Opinion Outlook*.

27   *Ibid.*

28   On the connection between American credibility and regional cooperation see Novik, *Encounter with Reality*.

29   See Chapter 1, above.

30   Anti-Israel lobbying has already attempted to suggest that aid to Israel was at the expense of "farmers, senior citizens, Vietnam veterans, small businessmen, health researchers, educators, even the U.S. defense [establishment]" all suffering from "belt tightening...by the Congress." A letter from Frederick Dutton, registered agent of Saudi Arabia, to members of Congress, April 18, 1983.

31   By FY 1982 Israel's payment of principal and interest reached $782 million. By FY 1983: $897 million; by FY 1984: $906 million. Abraham Tal, "The Annual Pilgrimage to Washington," *Ha'aretz*, Sept. 19, 20, 1983. See also Comptroller General, *US Assistance to the State of Israel* (Washington, DC: GAO), 1983, pp. 33, 37-38.

32   An exaggerated reflection of this new image can be found in the following report by a leading Washington-oriented publication: "For the first time in years, aid to Israel is almost as much a liability as an asset to the political fortunes of foreign aid legislation. The events in Lebanon...raised widespread questions about the extent of American economic and military support for Israel." John Felton, "Foreign Aid Issues Resolved," *Congressional Quarterly*, October 9, 1982, p. 2625.

33   See Chapter 2, above.

Chapter 6

1   David A. Deese and Joseph S. Nye, "Energy and Security," *Harvard Magazine*, January-February 1981, pp. 39c-40c.

2   Robert Stobough and Daniel Yergin, "The End of Easy Oil," as reported in *Economic Impact*, no. 3 (1980), p. 8.

3   As quoted in Lawrence Goldmuntz, "American Energy Politics," a paper

delivered at the Weitzman Institute International Seminar on Energy (Rehovot, Israel: The Weitzman Institute for Science) January 7, 1982, p. 5.

4   Central Intelligence Agency, National Foreign Assessment Center, *The World Oil Market in the Years Ahead* (Washington, DC: August 1979).

5   *The Effect of Oil Pricing On Output, Prices, and Exchange Rates in the United States and Other Industrialized Countries.* CBO (Washington, DC: February 1981), pp.103-107.

6   *New York Times*, February 29, 1980.

7   *Washington Post*, September 26, 1979.

8   *The Wall Street Journal*, February 29, 1980.

9   *Washington Post*, March 13, 1980.

10   See, for example, *Los Angeles Times*, March 17, 1980; *Washington Star*, April 23, 1980; *Long Island Newsday*, April 24, 1980; *The New Republic*, May 3, 1980; *Wall Street Journal*, May 14, 1980.

11   *Long Island Newsday*, April 24, 1980.

12   See Eliyahu Kanovsky, "The Diminishing Importance of Middle East Oil: A Harbinger of the Future?" in Colin Legum (ed.), *Middle East Contemporary Survey*, vol. 5 (1980-81) (London: Holmes & Meier, 1982), p. 373. New projections predicted continued decline in OPEC exports through the year 2000. *Middle East Economic Survey*, September 28, 1981, p. 9.

13   Donald O. Croll, "Continuing Slump in OPEC output," *Petroleum Economist*, January 1982, p. 5.

14   Kanovsky, "The Diminishing Importance," p. 373.

15   *National Journal*, July 10, 1982, p. 1231. During the same period, oil imports by members of the OECD declined 24%. *Dapei Meida* (Tel Aviv: Israel Institute for Petroleum and Energy), no. 50 (July 1, 1928), p. 6.

16   *Petroleum Economist*, January 1982, p. 30.

17   William A. Niskanen, "Energy Policy in the Reagan Administration" (unpublished monograph), February 3, 1983, p. 1.

18   *National Journal*, July 10, 1982, p. 1231.

19   *National Journal*, July 20, 1981, p. 1106; February 20, 1982, p. 325. See also Goldmuntz, "American Energy Politics," p. 12; *Congressional Quarterly*, January 7, 1984, p. 22.

20   According to US Secretary of Energy Don Hodel, US imports averaged 4.0 MBD by early 1983. In an interview published by *US News and World Report*, March 28, 1983, p. 21.

21   Niskanen, "Energy Policy in the Reagan Administration;" Brian Nutting, "Congress to Review US Plans for Meeting Energy Shortages," *Congressional Quarterly*, January 7, 1984, pp. 21-25.

22   *Dapei Meida* (Tel Aviv: Israel Institute for Petroleum and Energy), no. 53 (October 3, 1982), p. 4.

23   Kanovsky, "The Diminishing Importance," p. 373.

24   *National Journal*, July 20, 1981, p. 1106; February 20, 1982, p. 325.

25   See, for example, *Business Week*, May 25, 1981, p. 106. See also, Goldmuntz, "American Energy Politics;" Kanovsky, "The Diminishing Importance;" and Niskanen, "Energy Policy in the Reagan Administration," pp. 1-2.

26   William M. Brown, *Can OPEC Survive the Glut?* Hudson Institute Research Memorandum No. 112 (New York: October 1981), p. 1. For a similar analysis see also, Henry S. Rowen and John P. Weyant, "Will Oil Prices Collapse?" *Challenge*,

November-December 1981, pp. 11-17; S. Fred Singer, "What Do the Saudis Do Now?" *Wall Street Journal*, March 18, 1983, p. 26.

27 See the various experts quoted in "A Breather for Oil Prices," *Business Week*, May 25, 1981, pp. 104-115. See also the many corporate executives' reporting of changed long-term planning resulting from already declined oil prices and expectation of price stability in the future, as quoted in Robert D. Hershey, Jr., "How the Oil Glut is changing Business," *New York Times*, June 21, 1981.

28 Brown, *Can OPEC Survive?* p. 1.

29 *Business Week*, May 25, 1981, pp. 108, 115, respectively.

30 William Tucker, in *Harper's*, November 1981, pp. 25-36.

31 *Ibid.*, p. 36.

32 As reflected in such headlines as "New Hope for U.S. Energy Independence: OPEC Hold on World Has Loosened," *Washington Post*, June 15, 1981; or "Energy Crisis Appears Gone...", *New York Times*, March 10, 1982. See also, *The Wall Street Journal*, March 30, 1982; *New York Times*, June 21, 1981.

33 See, for example, Karen Elliott House's prediction that "...the soft oil market...promises to transform the psychology of Middle East politics by removing Arab oil as the central preoccupation of American policy." *The Wall Street Journal*, April 29, 1982. See also Youssef M. Ibrahim, "Oil's Use as a Political Weapon is Dead, US Executives, Arab Ministers Agree," *The Wall Street Journal*, October 1, 1982.

34 As quoted in *National Journal*, July 18, 1981, p. 1282.

35 National Energy Plan No. 3 (NEP III), a biennial report sent to Congress July 17, 1981, as quoted in *Congressional Quarterly*, August 1, 1981, p. 1424.

36 See, *Economic Report of the President* (Washington, DC: US Government Printing Office, 1983), particularly pp. 106-108.

37 In February 1981, less than one month after oil prices had been deregulated, 3500 oil rigs were in operation, one-third more than in 1980. *National Journal*, February 28, 1981, p. 364. In the first half of 1981, 16,000 oil wells were successfully drilled, 41.2% more than in 1980. *National Review*, February 19, 1982, p. 157.

38 *National Journal*, February 28, 1981, p. 364.

39 In a June 15, 1981 article, the *Washington Post* reported that many conservative and liberal experts alike shared a vision of upcoming American "total oil independence." The article pointed out that "the major dissenters [were] big oil companies like Exxon, whose executives see imports holding roughly steady into the next century..."

40 Interviews conducted by this author, Washington, DC, April, September 1981.

41 *Congressional Quarterly*, January 7, 1984, p. 21.

42 *The Geopolitics of Oil*, as reported in *National Journal*, December 6, 1980, p. 2089.

43 For a detailed study of these questions, see Eliyahu Kanovsky, "The Diminishing Importance," and "Saudi Arabia in the Red," *The Jerusalem Quarterly*, no. 16 (Summer 1980), pp. 137-144.

44 See, for example, Brian Nutting (1984), "Congress to Review," p. 21.

45 *National Journal*, February 20, 1982, p. 325. A more explicit list of pessimistic projections was suggested by Walter J. Levy, in his "Oil and the Decline of the West," *Foreign Affairs*, Summer 1980, p. 1015.

46 By mid-1982 Reagan administration officials were quoted as having concluded that "the shadow of the Arab oil weapon over American Mideast policy-making is

receding." *The Wall Street Journal*, April 29, 1982. By early 1983 a member of the administration's Council of Economic Advisers put it bluntly: "...an embargo threat against a specific nation...is empty." Niskanen, "Energy Policy in the Reagan Administration," p. 2.

47 *Ibid.*

48 See, for example, "The Leverage of Oil," by the editors of the Foreign Policy Association, as adopted in *Economic Impact*, no. 3 (1980), p. 17. These views were also expressed to this author by State Department and National Security Council officials interviewed in April and September 1981.

49 As reported in Benyamin Shwadran, "Will the Arabs impose an Embargo on the US?" *Ha'aretz*, August 16, 1982.

50 *Washington Post*, March 6, 1981.

51 US Dept. of Energy *Fact Sheet*, February 16, 1984. See also *Congressional Quarterly*, January 7, 1984, p. 22.

52 "Attitudes Concerning the American Jewish Community: The Gallup Poll, November, 1981," The American Jewish Committee (N.P.), December 1981, p. 1.

53 William J. Quirk, "Oil Dollars in America's Economy," *Newsday*, November 15, 1979. For similar views expressed by other popular publications, see Tucker in *Harper's*, November 1981, and *Penthouse Magazine*, April 1982.

54 Quirk in *Newsday*, November 15, 1979.

55 *The Operations of Federal Agencies in Monitoring, Reporting on, and Analyzing Foreign Investments in the United States (Part 2 – OPEC Investment in the United States)*, Hearing before the Subcommittee on Commerce, Consumer and Monetary Affairs, House Committee on Government Operations, July 1979, p. 78.

56 *Ibid.*, p. 80.

57 For a most thorough treatment of the subject, see Benjamin J. Cohen, "Financial Interests and US Foreign Policy in the Middle East," an unpublished manuscript (Mass: Tufts University), February 1982.

58 *Ibid,* p. 3.

59 *Ibid.*, p. 4.

60 *Ibid.* Another thorough study concluded that the figure was closer to $180 billion. See report of Steven Emerson press conference, *B'nai B'rith Messenger*, April 30, 1982. A lower figure of $78 million is suggested in Alan Stoga, "The Foreign Investments of OPEC and Arab oil producers," *American-Arab Affairs*, vol. 3, no. 1 (Winter 1982/3), p. 62.

61 See, for example, *The US-Saudi Relationship* (New York: ADL) Spring 1982, pp. 10-11; Louis J. Walinsky, *Arab Investments and Influence in the United States* (New York: American Jewish Committee), October 1978, p. 16.

62 Cohen, "Financial Interests," pp. 6-7.

63 Here, too, Cohen's analysis is most persuasive. *Ibid.*

64 US Senate Committee on Foreign Relations, *International Debt, the Banks, and US Foreign Policy*, A Staff Report (Washington, D.C., 1977), p. 8.

65 Cohen, "Financial Interests," p. 6.

66 *Ibid.*, p. 7.

67 Bank of America, Chase Manhattan, Chemical Bank, Citibank, Manufacturers Hanover, and Morgan Guaranty.

68 Cohen, "Financial Interests," p. 9.

69 See, for example, the takeover of an 11-bank US interstate holding company by a consortium from Saudi Arabia, Kuwait and the United Arab Emirates as reported

in the *Jerusalem Post*, March 4, 1982.

70 See, for example, Cohen, "Financial Interests," pp. 10-11; *Newsweek*, October 19, 1981, *Time*, October 19, 1981; *New York Times*, December 6, 1981; Stoga, "The Foreign Investments," p. 63.

71 *Ibid.* See also "New Kuwaiti Investment Stirs Controversy," *Petro Impact*, vol. 5, no. 1 (January 1982), p. 1.

72 Memo, L.F. McCollum to Walt Rostow, 22 June 1967, EX. NO 19/CO 1-6. WHCF, LBJ Library, Austin, Texas.

73 *New York Times*, December 22, 1969, *Business Week*, January 17, 1970. Present were David Rockefeller, president of the Chase Manhattan Bank; John J. McCloy, former president of the bank; Robert B. Anderson, director of Dresser Industries; Eugene Black, financial adviser to the government of Kuwait.

74 Findings of the Multinational Corporation Subcommittee of the Senate Foreign Relations Committee as reported in Steven Emerson, "Propaganda Pipeline," *The Jerusalem Post Magazine*, May 27, 1982, p. 5.

75 *Ibid.*

76 *Ibid.* See also Emerson's "The Petrodollar Connection," *The New Republic*, February 17, 1982, pp. 18-25; Fredelle Z. Spiegel, "The Arab Lobby," *Middle East Review*, vol. XIV, no. 1 (Fall 1981), pp. 69-73; *The US-Saudi Relationship*.

77 Emerson, "The Petrodollar Connection," p. 24.

78 For the involvement of such major corporations as the Fluor Corporation, see Tucker in *Harper's*, November 1981, p. 40.

79 One manifestation of Mobil's intimacy with the Saudi leadership was Riyadh's decision to hire Fred Dutton as its chief registered agent in Washington. It was at the recommendation of Rawleigh Warner, Chairman of the Board of Mobil, that Dutton was hired. See Karen Elliot House, "The Power Brokers," *Wall Street Journal*, March 29, 1982.

80 This series of advertisements ran through November 1981. See, for example, *New York Times, Washington Post,* August 27; October 13, 1981.

81 Frederick Dutton, Stephen N. Conner, and J. Crawford Cook.

82 Prince Bandar ibn Sultan (son of the Saudi Minister of Defense) and Abdullah Dabbagh.

83 *Los Angeles Times*, October 30, 1981.

84 For examples of these procedures, see *Christian Science Monitor,* June 8, 1981; *Wall Street Journal,* October 22 and October 30, 1981. For the findings of a most detailed investigation of this issue, see Emerson, "The Petrodollar Connection."

85 In a quarter-page "op-ed" placed in eleven major American newspapers during the second week of October 1981.

86 For an account of these three construction companies' dealings with Saudi Arabia and their political *quid pro quo*, see *Harper's Magazine*, July 1980, pp. 39-40.

87 See, for example, *New York Times*, August 27, 1981.

88 "US-Arab Trade," special feature in *Middle East Economic Digest* (MEED), October 1982, p. 6. See also William F. Lee, "US-Arab Economic Ties: An Interdependent Relationship," *American-Arab Affairs*, no. 3 (Winter 1982-3), pp. 7-9.

89 It is difficult to distinguish the share of OPEC-oriented major oil companies from that of the more domestically-oriented smaller companies. Yet it can be safely assumed that the former are at least as active in oil PACs as they are in the more

visible dimensions of political lobbying.

90   *Washington Post*, September 15, 1981.

91   For an account of Kuwaiti and Saudi involvement in the Idaho senatorial race, see Lee Gabow, "The Power of Money," *The Jerusalem Post*, May 12, 1983.

92   Robert Joseph, president of the National Association of Arab-Americans (NAAA) and of Middle East Policy and Research Corporation (MEPARC), as quoted in "US-Arab Trade," *MEED*, October 1982, p. 15.

93   Lee, "US-Arab Economic Ties," p. 5.

94   *Israel Today*, July 6, 1983.

95   Quoted in "US-Arab Trade," p. 6.

96   See Maj.Gen.(Res.) Aharon Yariv, "Regional Dynamics and Western Strategy," in Nimrod Novik and Joyce Starr (eds.), *Challenges in the Middle East* (New York: Praeger, 1981), pp. 1-8.

97   Save for occasional PLO threats to sabotage oil facilities and transporters.

98   On the relevancy of US security policy vis-à-vis the Persian Gulf to Israeli security, see Novik, *Addressing a Strategic Dilemma*.

99   See the conclusion to Chapter 5, above.